GW01087122

CHRISTY ZETTA KING

Inner Peace Architect

Title: Inner Peace Architect

"Designing a Life of Calm, One Moment at a Time"

Table of Contents

Part Three: Designing the Inner Sanctuary

Part Four: The Architect's Legacy

Part Five: Constructing Love

Dear Reader,

I welcome you into these pages as though inviting you into a sacred sanctuary, where the quiet stirrings of your soul have led you here. Something significant is calling within you—an inner voice seeking answers, solace, and transformation. Let me assure you, you are not alone in this journey. I, too, have walked a similar path, grappling with chaos, searching for peace, and yearning for a way to heal.

The challenges of life—the ones that push us to our limits—are what shaped these words. They emerge from my own struggles, which began when I was just a child. My early years were marked by a stark duality. On one side, there was my mother—a harbor of love and compassion, whose arms were a refuge of comfort. On the other side was my father—an unpredictable force whose presence loomed like a shadow over my world.

He did not live with us, having left before I was born, yet his visits were like the unsettling arrival of an unwelcome guest. His words cut sharply, often escalating into more than words. I vividly remember the sound of his hard-soled shoes echoing down the hallway, a sound that froze the air. My body would tense as if bracing for an unseen impact. Some days, his fury left physical marks; other days, it was the absence of kindness that weighed heavier.

In my teenage years, after a desperate cry for help led to a legal intervention, my father was removed from my life. For the first time, I experienced a sense of relief—a new chapter filled with laughter, friendships, and the unwavering love of my mother.

It seemed like peace had finally arrived. But as the years passed, I began to realize that the turmoil hadn't disappeared; it had merely taken root within me.

In my twenties, I saw the reflection of my father in myself—restless, angry, and reactive. My unresolved pain sabotaged relationships and left me estranged from the world. The only bond that remained was with my mother, but even she couldn't shield me from the turmoil inside. When she was diagnosed with cancer and eventually passed away, I felt untethered. The anger I carried became all-consuming, turning inward and outward in equal measure.

In the quiet of my grief, a painful truth surfaced: I was allowing my past to dictate my future. The echoes of my father's influence reverberated through my life, stealing not just my childhood but also my potential. I realized I had to make a choice—to let the past define me, or to reclaim my power and chart a new path.

That choice led me to meditation and spiritual teachings. I began to seek the stillness within, searching for the calm I desperately needed. I could never have imagined that this journey would lead me here—to a place where I could guide others through their own struggles.

And now, through these pages, I extend my hand to you. My story is not unique, but it is a testament to the possibility of transformation. Whatever challenges you face, know that healing is possible.

Peace is within reach. You are the architect of your own inner balance. Within this book, I share the techniques and insights that helped me rebuild from the inside out. These practices are designed not just to help you find calm but to cultivate a lasting foundation of inner strength.

So, let us begin this journey together. May these pages serve as a guide—a blueprint for rising above the challenges of life, not by avoiding them, but by transforming them into stepping stones. What lies ahead is not an end, but the beginning of a profound and powerful transformation.

Part One

Foundations of Inner Peace

Chapter One

Welcome to the Path of Inner Peace

In this age, we find ourselves standing on the cusp of remarkable times—times when spiritual practices are no longer luxuries but lifelines. The world is shifting, entering a new era so drastically different from what it was 30, 50, or even 100 years ago. Stress, once a personal burden to bear, has now expanded into something global, something woven into the very fabric of modern existence. It's as if the very pulse of the Earth hums with heightened tension, pressing down on each of us, making the air heavier, the days shorter, and the nights longer.

But this is not just about the weight of more information or technology; no, it's something far deeper. It's about the ever-growing demands placed upon your shoulders—the ceaseless call to be more, to achieve more, to stretch yourself thin across all corners of your life. In relationships, in careers, in the pursuit of personal growth, the expectations never seem to pause. The race never seems to slow. And here we are, asked to run faster, to carry more, to balance precariously in a system that feels ever more complicated.

In this whirlwind, even the sanctuaries of the heart—our relationships-are not spared. Look back, just a few generations. Our grandparents, perhaps your own, lived by the philosophy of "just endure." They faced hardships in marriage, in friendship, in life, but rarely did they consider walking away. Separation was not the solution; resilience was. And yet, today, the story is different. When the winds shift or our needs go unmet, we're quicker to let go. Friendships, once carved from stone, now dissolve like mist after a single disagreement. Marriages that once endured lifetimes now falter under the weight of fleeting discomforts.

Why has this changed?

It's not just the pace of life that has quickened. It's our tolerance for uncertainty that has diminished. We no longer carry the same reserves of patience, of acceptance, and this—this erosion of inner stillness—adds another layer to what I call the "stress quotient" of our time. In this new age, stress is no longer just a whisper in the background; it's a roaring companion, following us from morning to night, echoing in our heads and hearts.

In the past, jobs were stable havens. You could make mistakes, learn, and grow without the fear of immediate dismissal. Today, the ground beneath your feet feels less certain. One misstep, and the safety net disappears, leaving you vulnerable in a world that moves faster than ever. And so, stress grows, intertwining with the complexity of modern life.

But here, in the midst of this complexity, there is a silver thread—a return to ancient spiritual practices. Meditation, mindfulness, self-care—these are not just modern trends. They are ancient tools, once lost but now found again. They are essential, not just for surviving but for truly thriving in the chaos that surrounds us.

The Three Layers of Stress: Personal, National, and Global

Now, you might ask, "How can I manage not just my own inner turmoil but the weight of the world as well?" And this is where we must understand the layers of stress, each one intricately connected to the other like a set of nesting dolls.

At the very core, we find your personal stress—the smallest doll, closest to your heart. This is where your relationships, your career, your health, and your immediate world live. It's intimate, personal, and deeply felt. But surrounding that is the national stress, the second layer, where the pressures of taxes, healthcare systems, political events, and the state of your country begin to encroach on your life. Finally, there's the largest, outermost doll: global stress—the sweeping issues of wars, climate change, economic downturns, and global crises that ripple through all nations.

These layers are not separate; they are like tides, influencing one another. When your personal stress remains low, when your inner doll is calm, the outer layers—national and global—struggle to disturb you. But when the core of your being is already in turmoil, even the smallest tremor from the outside world can shake you to your core.

Have you ever noticed how some people become completely undone by global events or political changes, even when these events don't directly impact their lives? This happens when their personal stress is already teetering on the edge, and all it takes is one gust from the outer world to push them into the storm.

So, what is our goal? It's simple, yet profound. We must first bring your personal stress under control. We must calm the storm within. Once you master this, once your inner world is a place of peace, the external pressures—whether they come from your country or from the world at large—will feel like whispers in the wind, barely brushing against your calm.

Imagine this process like standing in the eye of a hurricane. All around you, chaos may swirl—world events, political unrest, personal struggles—but within the center, where you stand, there is stillness. A sacred stillness, unshaken by the world's noise.

And that is where we begin. Together, on this journey, we will build that stillness within you, layer by layer, until no storm can break through.

A Sacred Technique for Inner Healing: The Art of Sketching

Welcome to this part of the book, where we explore a special technique I've mentioned before—a gentle prelude to what's to come. This technique, known as "sketching," is one that our minds truly appreciate because it offers a visual, tangible way to understand and address what's happening in the body.

"Sketching" is more than just an artistic exercise. It's a method where you take what's hidden in your mind and body and bring it into the light. By drawing out your feelings and physical sensations, you give shape to what's often difficult to express. This ancient practice has roots in many healing traditions, where symbolic representations were used to understand the body's energy and balance.

Ancient Egyptian healers, for example, believed in the power of drawing to reveal the body's state. They would sketch symbols and figures representing areas of imbalance, using their visual interpretations to direct healing energy. Similarly, in the East, the body's meridians or chakras are mapped visually to help identify where blockages may exist. This visualization is key because it allows us to see what's often hidden.

What is Sketching?

The "sketching" technique I'll guide you through in this chapter allows you to visually map out what's happening in your body. Ideally, we'd use an image of your physical self, but for now, you'll create a representation—a drawing, a sketch that symbolizes your body. Through this drawing, you will quite literally identify and mark areas of concern. This isn't about addressing your manifestations, your soul, or even your relationships—this is purely about the body. It's about allowing your body to speak and guiding you toward healing it.

Imagine this process like a legend from ancient Greece, where the warrior Achilles was invincible except for his heel. Had Achilles been able to map out the weakness in his body, perhaps history would have told a different tale. You are now the architect of your own well-being, mapping out your strengths and vulnerabilities, and providing care to those areas that need it most.

You will draw, write, and circle areas of concern—places that feel tense, painful, or threatened. These could be physical sensations or simply places where you feel something is "off." You'll assess the level of risk—not for your manifestations, your desires, or your relationships, but for your body alone. Everything else becomes secondary in this moment. Because when your body is in a state of distress—whether it's panic attacks, anxiety, or physical tension—it's as though it's saying, "How can I give more when I'm already struggling?" In such moments, asking your body to focus on fulfilling your life's purpose or manifesting something new feels like asking too much. Your body needs peace and calm now, not future promises of well-being.

I can vividly recall those moments when even the smallest thing felt like the collapse of my entire world. It wasn't just fear—it was a deep, gut-wrenching panic that gripped every part of me. If something went wrong, no matter how trivial, my mind would spiral into the darkest of places. I truly believed that I would lose everything—be left starving, alone, abandoned, and possibly homeless. The thought of ending up on the streets, with no one to turn to, felt terrifyingly real.

These emotions weren't just whispers in the back of my mind; they were a tidal wave that crashed over me, drowning me in overwhelming fear. It was as if I had no control, no grounding—just a constant sensation that my life, as I knew it, was on the verge of complete destruction. I could barely breathe as these emotions wrapped themselves around my chest, suffocating any sense of logic or calm.

I thought, What if I lose everything? What if no one is there for me? What if I can't even find a way to feed myself? These weren't just fleeting thoughts—they felt like undeniable truths. My heart pounded as though I was in immediate danger, my stomach clenched with fear, and my body was on high alert, bracing itself for the worst possible outcome.

And yet, looking back, none of these fears ever came to pass. There was never any real danger of losing everything or ending up on the streets. But in those moments, my body didn't know that. To me, it was all too real. The threat, the devastation—it was as if the ground beneath my feet was crumbling, and I was helpless to stop it.

My body suffered deeply in the wake of these emotional tempests. Every muscle ached from the constant tension. My heart felt like it could burst from the intensity. It was as though my body was trapped in a prison of fear, holding on for dear life, trying to shield me from threats that didn't even exist. But to me, they were real. They were all too real.

This is where the wisdom of ancient spiritual practices comes into play. In the same way that Buddhist monks use mindfulness to bring awareness to each part of the body, we, too, will focus on the present moment—on what your body needs now, not what it should achieve later.

Chapter Two

Choosing the Right Meditation

Meditation is always the answer, yes. But the right meditation is essential. Imagine your body is experiencing turbulence, like the sea during a violent upheaval, and yet, you are asking it to focus on something grand like life's purpose. How do you think it will respond? It can't pull calm from future possibilities, no matter how bright. It needs peace right here, right now.

This is where the right meditation comes in. You need to choose meditations that heal, that focus on the immediate needs of your body. If you try to meditate on manifesting abundance while your body is in crisis, it's no surprise that your body resists. Your physical self is crying out for healing, not for future dreams. Offer it what it needs—calm, restoration, balance—and it will respond with gratitude.

The Power of Sketching in Healing

What exactly does this practice of sketching offer you?

When your entire system feels like it's under siege, calming everything at once seems impossible. It's like trying to steady a raging river by calming every rapid. Instead, we must find the weak link—the one area of your body that's struggling the most, pulling the rest down with it. This is the key to beginning the healing process. Much like the ancient architects and healers who understood that even the smallest cracks in the foundation needed immediate attention, you are now becoming the architect of your own well-being.

You start by drawing a representation of yourself—your body, or even a simple symbol that resonates with you. It doesn't need to be perfect or intricate; it just needs to speak to you.

Then, you begin marking the areas where you feel tension, pain, or tightness. Use colors, symbols, or shapes that match the intensity of these sensations. Imagine yourself as a wise healer from ancient times, mapping out the hidden parts of your inner world that are calling for your attention.

Now, as you do this, ask yourself these important questions:

- Could this stress be affecting my physical body?
- Is this tension interfering with my sleep?
- Does it disrupt my sense of security or stability?
- Do I feel disconnected from others because of this stress?
- Is my health or ability to take care of myself diminished by this tension?

Circle the areas of your body that respond to these questions. Pay attention to how your body reacts. Maybe your stomach tightens in response—mark that. Maybe your heart races, or your shoulders feel heavy with the weight of the world—acknowledge that.

Circle the areas of your body that respond to these questions. Pay attention to how your body reacts. Maybe your stomach tightens in response—mark that. Maybe your heart races, or your shoulders feel heavy with the weight of the world—acknowledge that.

By creating this visual map of your body's stress points, you now have a blueprint for where to direct your healing energy.

You don't need to try and heal everything at once. Instead, focus on these areas with intention, using meditations such as the Peaceful Breath Meditation or the Barometer Meditation—both of which I will guide you through in this book.

Each meditation is designed to target specific areas of tension, allowing your body to slowly but surely release the built-up pressure that has been holding you captive.

What is the likelihood of this?

Green means NOT LIKELY.
Yellow means SOME POSSIBILITY.
Red means VERY LIKELY.

Could I become hungry because of this?

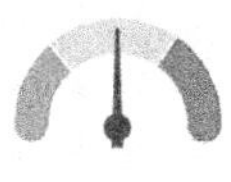

Could I lose my shelter or essential living necessities because of this?

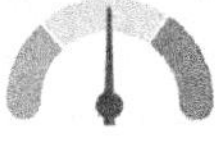

Could I lose all the people in my life because of this?

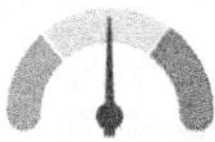

Could I lose my health because of this?

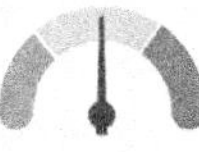

Could I lose my sleep because of this?

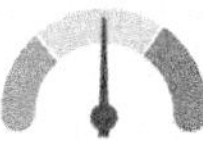

What does your body fear the most, according to the "barometer" levels above? Where is this stress being held in your body?

Breathe through it with the "Peaceful Breath" meditation, which I've written below, where you also invite the opposite of that fear. For example, if you're afraid of insomnia, visualize yourself sleeping peacefully...

Focusing on One Area at a Time

One of the reasons people often feel overwhelmed when they meditate is that they try to tackle everything at once. They attempt to calm their mind, emotions, and relationships simultaneously. But, much like a wise builder knows to reinforce one wall before moving to the next, you must focus on one area of your body at a time. By addressing that, you'll find peace ripples through the rest of your body.

When you sketch out your physical sensations and focus on a single area, you allow the body to speak its truth. This is not about complicating the process; it's about making it as simple and focused as possible. Start with one issue, one point of concern, and bring it into your Peaceful Breath Meditation or Barometer Meditation.

Even if two areas feel equally important, choose one for now. There will always be time to address the others. Let this focused meditation work its magic on your body.

The Peaceful Breath Meditation is your anchor, your go-to technique when your body is under intense physical or emotional pressure. It is the immediate release valve for all the stress that's been quietly building up. To begin, ask yourself a simple question: "How was my day today?" Reflect on your emotions, your thoughts, and how your body is reacting to the world around you. This one question can open up an internal dialogue, guiding you to the meditation you need most at that moment.

Some days, everything will flow with ease—no need for deep intervention. On those days, the Peaceful Breath Meditation will keep your energy balanced, your spirit light. But other days will feel more turbulent. Your body might already be in defense mode, your mind searching for an anchor. On those days, the Barometer Meditation becomes your refuge.

The Barometer Meditation helps you measure your internal weather—like an emotional barometer. Emotions are much like atmospheric pressure; they rise and fall, creating moments of intense storms and periods of peaceful calm.

This meditation allows you to track the shifts in your emotional and physical state, reminding you that you are the observer of these inner fluctuations. When you feel overwhelmed or notice your body reacting to stress, the Barometer Meditation becomes your vital tool to reset your system.

There are times when your body is already calming down, but a subtle dissonance lingers—a low-level signal from your body, whispering, "Something is still off." It could be a slight tightness in your chest, an unsettled feeling in your stomach, or a restlessness you can't quite identify.

At that moment, both your mind and body are working together to process the stress. This is where the Barometer Meditation shines, helping you recognize these early signs before they intensify.

Consider how, after facing difficult events—a breakup, illness, or loss—your brain eventually begins to reassure you. It reminds you, "We've been through this before. We've navigated these rough waters, and we've come out stronger." This is the wisdom that experience offers. You carry within you the proof that you can survive even the toughest times. This is where the Barometer Meditation comes into full effect.

The Barometer Meditation doesn't just help you release current stress; it draws on your past victories, bringing them into the present. It taps into your reservoir of resilience, gently reminding you that you have already overcome so much. The mind, ever seeking reassurance, finds peace in the knowledge that you are still here, still standing, despite the challenges you've faced. You are living proof that you can handle what life brings your way.

By recalling these past experiences, your mind begins to relax, signaling to your body that it is safe, that you've been here before, and you know how to move through it. With this shift, the tension starts to dissolve, and your body begins to release the stress it's been holding onto.

How This Mirrors Ancient Teachings

In Buddhism, there is a powerful teaching on impermanence, known as Anicca. It reminds us that nothing is permanent—not joy, not pain, and certainly not the challenges we face. Anicca teaches us to recognize the transient nature of all things, and this aligns perfectly with the Barometer Meditation. By focusing on the fact that you've overcome difficulties before and understanding that these current challenges will pass too, the meditation anchors you in the knowledge that nothing stays the same forever. The turbulence will settle, and peace will return.

Just as ancient sailors relied on the stars and trusted their instruments to guide them through restless seas, we must learn to trust our own inner compass. The Barometer Meditation is like a modern-day spiritual tool that helps you navigate the emotional waves of life. It's a reminder that, just as the stars guided mariners, your past experiences and inner wisdom guide you through your journey.

This meditation is especially beneficial for those who feel uneasy when they lack control. It works much like the methods used in Fear of Flying treatment centers, where theory is combined with practice. They explain how planes function, what each sound means, and what movements are normal. By the time passengers board, they may not have control over the flight, but their knowledge gives them peace. Similarly, the Barometer Meditation guides your mind through a process of gentle reassurance. It reminds you that, although you may not have control over everything, you've faced similar challenges before and emerged stronger. This knowledge soothes the mind, which in turn sends calming signals to the body.

When your mind becomes a sanctuary of peace, your body naturally follows. The tension begins to dissolve, and a profound stillness envelops you. This is the heart of the Barometer Meditation—it doesn't solely aim to ease the body but draws upon the mind's innate wisdom to restore balance and harmony to your entire being.

A Practice Rooted in Grace and Resilience

As you journey through this practice, remember that the tools you need are already within you. The turbulence will subside, the skies will brighten, and you will emerge stronger for having navigated them. The Barometer Meditation is a mystical yet deeply grounding practice that embodies both grace and resilience. Trust in its simplicity and depth, for it holds the power to transform.

In this sacred meditative space, you are not merely enduring—you are flourishing. You are alchemizing challenges into growth, turning rough waters into tranquil streams, and reshaping fears into profound understanding. The peace you seek resides within you, ready to ripple outward into every aspect of your life.
you, and you have the power to carry it forward into every corner of your life.

Barometer Meditation

• *Take a deep breath and allow the air to fill your lungs slowly. Let the gentle rhythm of your breathing calm your mind. Breathe in, breathe out. Feel how, with each breath, you start to relax more and more, from the top of your head down to the tips of your toes.*

• *As you continue to breathe deeply, the space around you begins to change. A sense of peace wraps around you, like a soft cocoon of light. You find yourself in a perfectly round space, almost like a small enchanted circle. Flowing gently around you, a delicate stream begins to appear, its waters whispering as they glide smoothly in a never-ending loop.*

• *The presence of this magical stream soothes you. It flows both around you and within you, calming every part of your body. You can feel the flow of energy inside you synchronizing with the water outside. Harmony, balance—it all becomes a gentle melody within you, and everything seems a little lighter, a little more at peace.*

• *In this tranquil moment, something curious appears above your head—a barometer, one you've never seen before. You notice that this barometer is under pressure. It's reacting to a specific situation that's been weighing on your mind. Take a moment to focus on your brain now. Breathe deeply and ask yourself, what is causing this pressure? What is making your barometer spike?*

• *Perhaps it's something from your past, a memory, a situation you've experienced before. Maybe it's not the exact same event, but the emotional weight feels familiar. Visualize that past moment. Remember how you once faced something similar, and how, in the end, you resolved it.*

• *Now, take that positive memory—the moment when you found peace or strength—and gently press it against the barometer. Let it absorb the reassurance from your past. Feel how the pressure starts to ease, how the tension melts away. You'll notice your entire body softening, releasing every last bit of stress.*

• *And in this moment, remind yourself: You can do this. Everything will be alright. You've faced challenges before, and you've overcome them. You are strong, capable, and experienced.*

• *Feel the warmth of this realization fill you from within. It is like an old friend, returning to remind you that you are never truly alone in this journey. The pressure on the barometer subsides completely, and with it, a deep, profound peace washes over you.*

• *Let this peace linger, knowing that from now on, no situation can scare you anymore. You carry the strength of your past within you, and that gives you the courage to face anything.*

• *As this deep sense of calm takes root, you will feel it spreading through every part of your life. And when you open your eyes, you will carry this serenity with you—a peaceful rhythm that will guide you through every new moment.*

The Peaceful Breath Meditation

• *Close your eyes, and allow yourself to settle into this moment of peace.*

• *In your mind, softly repeat the word "peace."*

• *Peace. In every place. You deserve peace. And at this moment, you can embrace it fully.*

- *Shift your focus entirely to your breathing.*

- *As you do, you find yourself seated in a serene and almost magical place.*

- *Picture yourself in a gentle boat, gliding through still waters, surrounded by quiet beauty. The boat carries you calmly, peacefully. You don't know the exact destination, but it feels safe, comforting, and you surrender fully to the journey.*

- *Your only task now is to relax, breathe, and enjoy the soothing, peaceful ride.*

- *With each inhale, you take in the fresh air. And with each exhale, you release any tension held in your body.*

- *There is nothing you need to fix, nothing you need to worry about—just you and this calm, steady boat guiding you.*

- *In this quiet space, the air begins to feel lighter. You notice a gentle breeze starting to swirl around you, carrying with it a sense of healing.*

- *It's as if the breeze itself holds a kind of magical wisdom. It wraps around you, lifting you ever so slightly off the ground, giving you the sensation of floating—light, free, and entirely at peace.*

- *You feel the weight of the world slowly melt away. The heaviness you've carried is gone. You are no longer burdened. It's as if the winds are carrying all your worries far away, leaving you feeling lighter, more at ease.*

- *As you breathe deeply, you begin to see the outlines of peace forming all around you. These outlines are the opposite of anything that has troubled you. They are gentle, soft shapes representing calmness, tranquility, and love.*

- *As you continue to breathe, these outlines of peace begin to gravitate toward a small magnet in your heart—a healing magnet that gently pulls peace into the deepest corners of your being.*

- *The peace begins to flow through your body, reaching every place that once held tension. The outlines of peace fill your weak spots, transforming them into sources of strength.*

- *Your body, once tense, is now flooded with this peaceful energy. You can feel it moving through your lungs, your chest, your arms, and down into your legs. Every part of you becomes lighter, brighter, and filled with a gentle, quiet strength.*

- *As you take each breath, the outlines of peace travel deeper within you, and soon, you feel as though your entire body is glowing with calm. There is no place left untouched by this peace.*

- *Now, let this peace spread through your life. Picture yourself carrying this newfound calm into every corner of your day—your relationships, your thoughts, your actions. This peace is yours to keep, to draw upon whenever you need it.*

- *When you count down from ten to one, you will open your eyes feeling refreshed, grounded, and ready to carry this peace forward.*

- *10... 9... 8... You feel the light energy filling your body, grounding you back into the earth.*

- *7... 6... 5... The peace surrounds you and fills every cell of your being.*

- *4... 3... 2... Gently touch the spot where you once felt tension, but which is now a source of strength. Give it a soft pat, a sense of pride, for you've transformed it.*

- *1... Open your eyes.*

And remember, dear one, you always deserve peace!

Chapter Three

The Power of Sacred Questions: Rewiring the Mind for Peace

Do you remember how I shared the ways our bodies can spiral into stress, creating a cycle that magnifies tension? It's as if a wildfire ignites within us, spreading between our physical and emotional states until the intensity feels unbearable. Yet, there's another layer to this—one that lies hidden within the intricate pathways of our minds.

This deeper layer is where our thoughts and beliefs subtly fuel the flames, either escalating the chaos or dampening it. It's here that the Barometer Meditation works its magic, helping us navigate the complexity of our inner world, extinguishing the unrest, and cultivating a steady sense of calm. By addressing not only the fire but also the spark that started it, this practice brings harmony back to every part of your being.

For many of us, the mind becomes loud, full of chatter, especially when stress enters the picture. We're wired for this internal dialogue, and most people experience a constant hum of thoughts—thoughts that seem impossible to quiet. Yet, I've heard of rare souls who claim to live in a state of pure mental silence. They say they experience no inner noise, no self-talk at all.

I can barely imagine that!

For me—and perhaps for you, too—my mind is always alive. It's always engaged, whether I'm recalling a memory, being inspired by an angelic whisper, or simply thinking of the next task at hand. There's a rhythm to this constant activity, and much of the time, it's positive. But the idea of no thoughts at all? That seems like an unreachable paradise.

Most of us, though, feel that inner chatter growing even louder when stress approaches. It's as if our minds rush to fill every silence with questions: "What if everything falls apart? What if I fail? What if people judge me?" These questions can quickly snowball, creating a loop of fear, a spiral that pulls us deeper into anxiety. And this is where it becomes dangerous—we unintentionally start to manifest from this space of fear.

We know that thoughts shape our reality, a truth widely accepted in modern spiritual teachings. Many New Age practices advise countering negative thoughts with positive affirmations. We're encouraged to tell ourselves, "Everything is fine," or "The Universe has my back." But what happens when those positive affirmations feel hollow, when they seem to clash with the deeply ingrained fears?

The Struggle of Mismatched Energies

Imagine being trapped in the thought, "What if everything falls apart?" and trying to respond with "Everything is fine." These two energies don't align. They're like oil and water—they refuse to blend, no matter how hard you stir. It feels forced, doesn't it?

Some people manage to balance their negativity with layers of positivity, but for many of us, it feels like putting soda on cereal—it just doesn't work! Instead of soothing the mind, the positivity clashes with the fear, leaving us feeling more unsettled.

For those of us who struggle with this mismatch of energies, there's another way—one that feels more natural, more aligned with the energy of the situation.

The Power of Sacred Questions

This technique is one I've channeled specifically for this purpose: Sacred Questions. It's a beautifully simple yet transformative practice. Instead of forcing affirmations that feel out of place, we use the power of questions to gently shift the energy.

Questions, in themselves, are incredibly powerful. They direct the mind's focus, shaping the energy we dwell in. When we ask negative questions like, "What if I fail?" we're pulling ourselves into a downward spiral. But instead of trying to push positivity where it doesn't fit, we can shift our approach by asking a positive question about the same situation.

This is where Sacred Questions shine. Instead of battling negative thoughts with affirmations that feel forced, we pose new, open-ended questions that suggest positive outcomes without demanding immediate answers. For example, instead of thinking, "What if this goes wrong?" ask yourself, "What if this situation leads to my success?" or "What if this experience helps me grow?"

These questions don't require answers. They gently invite new energy into your mind, allowing your thoughts to settle into a more peaceful space without the pressure of resolution.

A Practice Rooted in Ancient Wisdom

The practice of Sacred Questions is deeply rooted in ancient spiritual traditions. In early Tibetan Buddhism, monks were taught to observe their thoughts as passing clouds—neither grasping nor pushing them away.

This practice wasn't about forcing positivity, but about allowing thoughts to flow freely, unattached to their outcomes. Over time, this led to a state of inner calm.

Similarly, in hypnotherapy, practitioners guide the mind toward relaxation using open-ended suggestions. Questions like, "What if peace is already within you?" allow the mind to drift into a place of ease without the pressure of finding answers.

Sacred Questions work in much the same way. They gently bypass the need for stressful answers, offering your mind a chance to rest in possibility, rather than fear. The mind no longer needs to frantically search for solutions; instead, it can simply float in the peace of what could be.

Anchoring Peace Through Sacred Questions

In the meditation I've created, you'll explore these Sacred Questions. You'll gently ask yourself, "What if this challenge is a stepping stone to my dreams?" or "What if this moment is the key to unlocking my highest potential?" These questions allow your mind to shift from fear to curiosity, inviting peace into your being without forcing any conclusions.

This technique is particularly helpful for those of us who crave control. We often feel the need to "figure it all out," to have the answers to every question. But with Sacred Questions, we release that pressure. We plant seeds of possibility and watch them grow, without needing to control how they'll bloom.

Here's a beautiful metaphor: imagine your mind is a garden. The negative thoughts are like stubborn weeds. Instead of pulling them out aggressively, you plant new seeds of Sacred Questions. Over time, these new thoughts grow, gently overshadowing the weeds, transforming your mind into a sanctuary of peace.

Creating a Bubble of Peace

For an extra layer of protection, gently place your hands over your ears during meditation. This act creates a symbolic barrier between you and the world's noise—the doubts, fears, and chatter. It tells your mind and body, "I'm in a sacred space now. I'm safe here."

This simple gesture can have a profound impact, creating a sanctuary within yourself. You'll find that the negative thoughts can't penetrate this space, and the positive energy of your Sacred Questions will begin to flow.

The Transformative Power of Sacred Questions

Remember, you don't need to find answers to these Sacred Questions. Let them drift through your mind, like leaves floating gently on a stream. Allow their peaceful energy to settle within you, replacing fear with curiosity, and anxiety with possibility.

And here's the secret: your soul didn't come into this world asking, "What if I fail?" These negative questions were learned over time. But now, with Sacred Questions, you can return to your soul's wisdom, a place where peace is your natural state.

This is the beginning of true transformation—where your inner world becomes a sanctuary of calm, and where every question holds the potential for peace.

This is where peace begins.

The Power of Sacred Questions - Meditation

- *Close your eyes.*

- *Begin by gently repeating a soft, natural breath.*

- *Feel the calm energy beginning to wrap around you, like a soothing breeze lifting you from within.*

- *It will carry you away to a fragrant, golden field of wheat.*

- *In this peaceful field, the tall wheat sways gently, exuding a serene and soft energy.*

- *The wind, like a tender embrace, caresses your body, carrying away all your thoughts and tensions.*

- *Here, among the swaying wheat, you become one with nature.*

- *The calm energy settles deeply into you, filling every part of your being with complete tranquility.*

- *You realize that this world has been created just for you.*

- *Above, you see the most beautiful clouds, drifting peacefully in the vast sky.*
- *These clouds represent your feelings of serenity. Perhaps they are light and*

bright, or maybe they carry a magical hue, with colors beyond what you've ever imagined.

- *Whatever they look like, these clouds bring a deep and lasting peace to your entire being.*

- *Simply observe the clouds, as the gentle wind continues to sweep away any remaining tension.*

- *With each breath, your body becomes more relaxed, more at peace, and even more still.*

- *And then, suddenly...*

- *A large, floating umbrella begins to drift down towards you from the clouds.*

- *It hovers above you, creating a field of safety, and you feel completely secure under this magical umbrella.*

- *As you look up, the umbrella takes on a color that is uniquely yours—a hue that reflects the essence of your soul.*

- *You know that now you are wrapped in a space that belongs to you alone.*

- *Now, gently place your hands over your ears.*

- *Feel how, by doing this, you create a special inner world, one that is entirely your own.*

- *Focus on this quiet space. What will begin to rain down from this umbrella?*

- *Because from this magical umbrella, a gentle rain begins to fall upon your body.*

- *But this is not just any rain. It rains questions.*

- *Questions, like tiny droplets of words, gently falling down, one by one.*

- *They enter your mind, softly traveling into every cell, and through your entire being.*

- *These are the questions.*

- *Questions connected to what has been causing you the most stress recently.*

- *You remember what it is, just for a brief moment.*

- *But as soon as you do, the questions begin to rain down, soothing you with their wisdom.*

- *Feel them. Absorb them into your body, into your heart, into your soul.*

- *"What if this is happening so I can move forward?"*

- *"What if this is the path to my dreams and desires?"*
- *"What if this will help me succeed in all areas of my life?"*
- *"What if this is an intervention from my soul?"*
- *"What if this is because my energy is truly powerful?"*
- *"What if this is happening because I'm doing something right?"*
- *"What if this is the activation of my advanced ethereal gifts?"*

- *Now, suddenly, you see these questions glowing inside of you, radiating peace and possibility.*

- *Then, the wind gently blows again.*

- *The umbrella begins to spin softly above you.*

- *It swirls, sending the glowing questions back into the space of waking reality.*

- *You gently lower your hands from your ears, feeling the energy of the questions integrating into your being.*

- *And in 4... 3... 2... 1... you slowly open your eyes.*

- *Trust that the programming has done its work.*

Let the power of these Sacred Questions carry you into a space of peace and transformation.

Part Two

Building Blocks of Harmony

Chapter Four

Navigating the Chaos of Emotions: A Journey of Inner Mastery

In the first part of this book, you learned how to manage daily stress—whether it comes from work, responsibilities, or simply the fast pace of life. These moments of stress can feel like walking on a tightrope, where one wrong move could send everything tumbling. But with the right tools, finding your calm becomes possible. Yet, life doesn't always present such manageable stress.
Sometimes, a single emotion erupts like a ticking time bomb, setting off a chain reaction that throws everything into disarray.

This is where the concept of the "chaos of emotions" comes into play—a state where one intense feeling acts like a spark hitting dry tinder. Once ignited, it pulls other emotions into its orbit, creating a cascading wave of inner turmoil. It's no longer just stress; it transforms into a wildfire, blazing through your sense of stability and leaving you feeling as if you're stranded in the heart of a maelstrom, desperately grasping for solid ground.

In these moments, it's easy to feel overwhelmed, as though you're battling an unstoppable force. But this is precisely where practices like the Barometer Meditation become invaluable. By gently redirecting your focus, it helps you step out of the chaos and reclaim control. Instead of being swept away by the flood of emotions, you learn to anchor yourself, allowing the storm to subside and clarity to emerge from within.

Misunderstanding the Role of Emotions

Have you ever heard someone dismiss another as "emotionless"? Let me tell you—this is an impossibility. Emotions may be buried, hidden deep within, but they are always there, quietly shaping a person's reality. To lack emotion is to lack a soul, and that simply cannot be.

The real danger lies not in feeling too much, but in suppressing what you feel. Suppressed emotions are like seeds planted in the dark; they grow in silence, twisting through your energy, your health, your very sense of self, until they manifest in ways you can no longer ignore.

The Myth of Negative Thoughts and Illness

Let's confront a popular myth head-on: negative thoughts alone do not create illness. Despite the widespread belief that negativity is a one-way ticket to disease, science tells a more nuanced story. Studies show that the average human has between 50,000 and 70,000 thoughts per day, and approximately 70% of them are negative.

If negative thinking were enough to doom us, we would see humanity collapsing under the weight of its own thoughts. Yet, that's not what happens. Even children, who often express frustration, fear, or sadness loudly and freely, are not burdened by chronic illnesses caused by these outbursts. Why?

Children are emotionally unfiltered. Their reactions are immediate and unrestrained, but they are not tethered to deeper emotional blockages. Their souls remain radiant, connected to an inherent love and purity that protects them from negativity's deeper effects.

Adults, however, are another story. As we age, we learn to suppress, to hide, to bury. This is where emotions turn toxic—not in their existence but in their suppression.

Spiritual practices have shown remarkable potential to create profound shifts in our mental and emotional landscapes.

Because emotions serve as a bridge to our deeper energy, once you understand and nurture this connection, the transformation becomes undeniable. Many who engage in emotional and spiritual practices report an extraordinary change—a rebalancing of thought patterns.

Imagine this: instead of the typical 70% of thoughts being negative and only 30% positive—a statistic often associated with daily mental habits—you could reverse this balance entirely. With consistent spiritual and emotional work, you can nurture a mindset where 70% of your daily thoughts shine with positivity, leaving just 30% in the shadows.

Oh yes, hallelujah, hallelujah!

It's as if the heavens themselves join in celebration. And perhaps you, too, will feel that pull—the realization that such change is not only desirable but entirely possible. Those who embrace spirituality, emotional growth, and inner exploration often find their lives reflecting this remarkable shift.

This isn't just for dreamers or the unconventional. These practices are accessible tools that can reshape your inner world and elevate your sense of balance and peace. They aren't just transformative—they're life-changing.

So, let's explore the possibilities. Imagine waking up to a life where the majority of your thoughts bring light and clarity. It's closer than you think.

Spirituality as Emotional Alchemy

Here lies the power of spirituality: it is the art of turning emotional chaos into clarity. Emotions are the bridge to your soul, and spirituality is the map that guides you across it.

Research in neuroscience and psychology supports this truth. Emotional awareness, coupled with spiritual practices like meditation or mindfulness, rewires the mind. It is not just anecdotal—it is transformative.

Individuals who once lived with predominantly negative thought patterns (up to 70% negative) have shown a profound shift. With intention and practice, they begin to live with thoughts that are predominantly positive—70% light, 30% shadow.

thoughts that are predominantly positive—70% light, 30% shadow. This is the alchemy of the soul. When you reconnect with your emotions, when you allow them to speak their truth, you shift the trajectory of your life. And yes, it feels like a Hallelujah moment.

Emotions Are Not Optional

Your emotions are not an accessory—they are your foundation. They are not a distraction but a compass pointing you toward your truth. They are the language of the soul, guiding you toward purpose, peace, and power.

To embrace your emotions is to embrace yourself. It is to walk hand in hand with your soul, trusting that every feeling—whether joy or sorrow, love or fear—is a step on the path to your ultimate becoming. This is the gift of being human: to feel deeply, to live fully, and to honor the sacred wisdom that lies within.

Those whispers that have told you your emotions are "too much." Oh, you're too emotional, they say. Your emotions control you too much. Do you know how many people I hear saying such things?

"Christy," they tell me, "I need to fix myself. I'm too emotional."

That phrase—I'm too emotional—is dangerous. Utterly dangerous. It's a declaration of war on your own essence. Because when you say you're too emotional, what you're really saying is this: I want to suppress my emotions.

But here's the truth: being too emotional is a myth. It doesn't exist. Saying you're too emotional is no different than saying, "I have too much soul." Would you ever tell someone to strip part of their soul away because it's too much? Of course not. And yet, that's exactly what you're suggesting when you decide your emotions are excessive.

You see, emotions are your soul's language. To say you have too many emotions is to say you have too much soul energy. And here's the kicker: emotions aren't just about sadness or anger—they're also the birthplace of your joy, your ecstasy, your profound moments of happiness.

So, if you suppress your so-called "negative" emotions, you're also muting the positive ones. Want to rid yourself of anger? Well, be ready to lose joy. Want to dull your sadness? Say goodbye to that radiant feeling of bliss. Because emotions don't work in isolation—they are a spectrum, interconnected, inseparable.

Now, let me ask you this: If I took away your ability to feel emotions, what would remain of your life? Without emotions, there is no joy. Without emotions, there is no passion, no love, no radiance. And without emotions, there is no manifestation.

You cannot create a life of beauty, abundance, or meaning without your emotions. They are the fuel, the driving force, the alchemy that transforms your desires into reality. Without them, you lose the spark that makes manifestation possible.

So, no.

I will not strip your emotions away. I would rather teach you to embrace them, to understand them, to navigate their power than take away even an ounce of what makes you whole.

It is far better to feel deeply—even painfully—than to feel nothing at all. The depth of your emotions is not a flaw; it is a masterpiece, crafted by your soul for a reason.

Emotions are not something to fix or diminish; they are a sacred system, designed by your soul itself. Just as your mind is wired for logic, your emotions are wired for meaning. They hold the keys to your growth, your purpose, your manifestation, and your destiny.

So, hear me when I say this: Your emotions are a blessing. They are not too much. They are everything.

And if anyone has ever made you feel otherwise, know this—it is not natural to stifle emotions. When people suppress their feelings, they lose the ability to feel deeply, to dream passionately, to embrace life fully. But this isn't your natural state.

You were born to feel. To love. To hope. To manifest. And your emotions? They are not a burden. They are your gift. Never forget that.

We have emotions because they are the fire that fuels motivation—

the sacred spark that moves us from mere existence to boundless creation.

Motivation is not born in the mind. It doesn't emerge from logic or cold calculation. It is forged in the furnace of emotions. Without emotions, motivation simply cannot exist. The brain alone is a master of structure and survival, but it is utterly lifeless without the vibrant pulse of emotional energy to give it purpose.

Let me show you what I mean:

Imagine presenting your brain with a mechanical instruction manual: "Here's the plan. You will work 18 hours a day, relentlessly completing tasks. Eventually, you'll have a significant amount of money, an expansive customer base, and the ability to purchase your dream home."

Does this inspire the brain? Not at all. Because to your brain, these concepts—money, customers, even the so-called "dream house"—are just empty data points. They lack the gravity to create action. They don't inspire urgency or passion.

Now, consider this: will this lifeless information be enough to push you through exhaustion, to keep your focus razor-sharp, to carry you over the obstacles that life inevitably throws your way? Not without the driving force of emotion. It's the emotional system—the deep, burning desire for change, success, or fulfillment—that ignites action.

The brain is an informational system, designed to collect and analyze. It is not, and never has been, the seat of motivation. Motivation is birthed in the emotional core of who you are.

You need something to ignite you—something that excites you enough to work tirelessly, even 18 hours a day. That drive doesn't come from logic or reasoning; it comes from joy, passion, and the emotional spark that fuels you. Without it, the brain simply cannot sustain action.

Have you ever had something in your life that thrilled you so much, you couldn't wait to throw yourself into it? Something that made your heart race and your energy soar? That's the power of emotions. Without that feeling, no amount of reasoning or planning could compel your brain to act. The emotional factor must be high enough to drive motivation.

Think about your children, if you have them. You might try to reason with them, saying, "You need to study now because when you're 30, you'll be grateful you did." But does that logic move a 13-year-old?

Hardly. To a child, the idea of a reward 17 years in the future is meaningless. Yet, if that same child passionately wants something—like a new bike or the freedom to pursue their dreams—they'll move mountains to achieve it. That's the emotional engine at work, and it's the same for all of us.

Why Suppression Harms Both the Body and the Soul

The societal pressure to suppress emotions has devastating consequences. When emotions are buried rather than expressed, they do not simply disappear—they fester. Over time, they manifest as physical ailments or erupt in moments of crisis when we least expect it.

For example, think of a memory that involved deep emotion—perhaps the loss of a loved one or an overwhelming moment of joy. These memories linger not because of their factual content but because of the emotional imprint they left behind. A passing encounter with a white dog might be forgotten unless it reminds you of a dog you've lost, triggering days of tears and introspection.

Unprocessed emotions don't just disappear; they wait for a moment to resurface. If they remain repressed for too long, they can erupt in overwhelming ways, destabilizing our lives. This is why learning to process emotions is essential—not just for emotional health but for physical and spiritual well-being.

The Collective Fear of Emotional Intensity

As a society, we've been taught to fear emotional intensity. Why? Because intense emotions demand attention, action, and transformation. It's easier for the collective to manage individuals who are "rational" and "calm" rather than those who are deeply expressive.

Think about how we react to someone crying, trembling with rage, or laughing uncontrollably. Their intensity demands a response, a disruption of the status quo. This is why we are conditioned to suppress emotions—because they challenge the collective's comfort zone.

But suppression comes at a cost. It disconnects us from our kindred souls, our values, and, ultimately, ourselves. When we suppress emotions, we suppress our ability to channel our desires, connect deeply with others, and align with our higher purpose.

A Call to Emotional Mastery

The goal is not to suppress emotions but to understand and channel them. Intense emotions—be they grief, anger, or joy—are not flaws to fix but energies to work with. They reveal what matters to us, where our boundaries lie, and what we're meant to pursue.

When you feel overwhelmed by emotions, don't wish them away.

Instead, view them as messengers, guiding you toward greater self-awareness and alignment. Seek environments and practices, like meditation or emotional workshops, where you can safely explore and express these feelings.

Imagine attending an emotional "school," where you learn not to fear your feelings but to embrace them. Better to confront and process your emotions deliberately than to have them ambush you unprepared.

Because here's the truth: emotions are your most profound ally in this journey called life. They are the threads that weave your relationships, the fire that fuels your dreams, and the compass that keeps you aligned with your soul's purpose.

So, the next time you feel the surge of emotion—whether it's joy, anger, or sadness—welcome it.

Listen to it. Let it guide you. Because your emotions are not your weakness; they are your strength.

The Overflowing Glass: Understanding Emotional Overload

Think of your emotional system as a glass of water. A healthy emotional system is like a balanced, steady glass—it can hold new emotions and challenges without spilling over. When a significant emotional experience arises, it processes and releases it, leaving the glass stable and ready for the next.

But what happens when your glass is already full?

Many of us carry unresolved emotions from the past—old wounds, unspoken words, unprocessed grief. These sit in our glass, filling it up drop by drop. When something new occurs, even a small emotional trigger, it's like adding more water to an already brimming glass. That's when the overflow happens, and we feel overwhelmed or unable to cope.

Healthy Emotional Systems vs. Overflowing Glasses

A healthy emotional system operates differently. When past emotions have been addressed and healed, the system remains stable, even in moments of emotional intensity. A single strong emotion won't break you, disrupt your health, or shatter your circumstances because the system can handle isolated intensity.

But if your glass is already overflowing with suppressed emotions, a new wave—no matter how small—can feel catastrophic. It tips the balance, leaving you unable to process or function effectively. This is how emotional breakdowns, depression, or anxiety often begin.

One Drop Too Many: A Story of Emotional Contrasts

Let me share a compelling example to illustrate this.

Imagine two people facing the same situation—they both lose their jobs unexpectedly. One person spirals into despair, convinced it's the end of the world. The other remains calm, viewing it as an opportunity to start anew. What makes the difference?

It's not the situation itself. The difference lies in their internal emotional systems.

The first person carries a history of unresolved pain, self-doubt, or fear. Their glass was already full, so this new event becomes the tipping point. The second person, however, has a healthier emotional system—one that's been processed and cleared of past baggage. They can absorb the challenge without breaking down.

How to Recognize and Heal Your Full Emotional Glass

1. Identify your suppressed emotions.

These are often the thoughts or feelings you avoid because they seem too painful or overwhelming to confront.

2. Face them, one step at a time.

Awareness is the first step. Journaling, meditation, or speaking with a trusted confidant can help create space to process them.

3. Accept emotional intensity as part of the healing process.

Suppressed emotions will feel powerful when they surface. Allowing them to flow freely will eventually bring clarity and calm.

Healthy Emotional Systems vs. Overflowing Glasses

A healthy emotional system operates differently. When past emotions have been addressed and healed, the system remains stable, even in moments of emotional intensity. A single strong emotion won't break you, disrupt your health, or shatter your circumstances because the system can handle isolated intensity.

But if your glass is already overflowing with suppressed emotions, a new wave—no matter how small—can feel catastrophic. It tips the balance, leaving you unable to process or function effectively. This is how emotional breakdowns, depression, or anxiety often begin.

One Drop Too Many: A Story of Emotional Contrasts

Let me share a compelling example to illustrate this.

Imagine two people facing the same situation—they both lose their jobs unexpectedly. One person spirals into despair, convinced it's the end of the world. The other remains calm, viewing it as an opportunity to start anew. What makes the difference?

It's not the situation itself. The difference lies in their internal emotional systems.

The first person carries a history of unresolved pain, self-doubt, or fear. Their glass was already full, so this new event becomes the tipping point. The second person, however, has a healthier emotional system—one that's been processed and cleared of past baggage. They can absorb the challenge without breaking down.

How to Recognize and Heal Your Full Emotional Glass

1. Identify your suppressed emotions.

These are often the thoughts or feelings you avoid because they seem too painful or overwhelming to confront.

2. Face them, one step at a time.

Awareness is the first step. Journaling, meditation, or speaking with a trusted confidant can help create space to process them.

3. Accept emotional intensity as part of the healing process.

Suppressed emotions will feel powerful when they surface. Allowing them to flow freely will eventually bring clarity and calm.

What Science and Psychology Say

Neuroscientific research and psychological studies confirm that chronic emotional suppression increases the risk of mental health issues such as anxiety and depression. On the other hand, expressing and processing emotions—whether through therapy, art, or movement—activates brain regions that reduce stress and enhance resilience.

Antonio Damasio, a renowned neurologist, has shown in his work that emotions are not just feelings but integral mechanisms for decision-making and navigating life. They are the bridge between intuition and our deeper values, guiding us toward a fulfilled existence.

The Emotional Core of Connection

Emotions are also vital for communication, particularly with kindred souls. Imagine if we all spoke in monotone voices, with robotic precision, devoid of any emotional expression. We would lose all sense of what's truly happening beneath the surface—what someone's energy is saying beyond their words.

For example, if someone calmly says, "I'm upset because you didn't mow the lawn," it might barely register. But if they raise their voice, tear up, or show visible frustration, it grabs your attention on a deeper level. You feel their emotion, and it compels you to respond, to care, to act.

This is why emotions are the foundation of relationships. They allow us to sense the needs of the souls we're connected to, whether it's resolving an issue or simply offering support. Without emotions, connections wither, and relationships—be they romantic, familial, or professional—start to crumble.

Why Emotionless Relationships Fail

So many people say they want partners or colleagues who are "calm" and "low-maintenance"—those who never complain, never express frustration, and are always agreeable. But let me tell you: those aren't the relationships that last.

Without emotional expression, there is no dynamic connection. A relationship built on robotic interactions will eventually fall apart, even if it's held together by shared assets, children, or routines.

When emotional expression is absent, sadness creeps in, followed by emptiness. You might hear someone say, "Well, at least we have a house, three kids, and a dog." But that's not a bond—it's a contract. Without emotional connection, the joy fades, and even the best foundations begin to crack.

Emotions Shape Your Values

Emotions also play a critical role in defining and defending your values. When your value system is challenged, it's your emotions that rise to protect it. That surge of passion or anger isn't random; it's your inner compass ensuring you stand firm for what matters most. Think about it—when you feel strongly about justice, fairness, or love, you become a powerful advocate. That intensity is what drives change, builds legacies, and forges unshakable connections with others.

And that's exactly as it should be. Your emotions are not a burden—they're your most profound strength.

The Science Behind Emotional Overload

• Dr. Gabor Maté, a renowned expert in trauma and stress, emphasizes that unprocessed emotional pain is often a root cause of chronic illnesses. He explains, "When the body says no, it's because the emotional self hasn't been heard."

• The brain's amygdala processes emotions, particularly fear and anger. When overwhelmed, the amygdala becomes hyperactive, triggering fight-or-flight responses even in situations that don't warrant such reactions.

• Emotional processing helps reduce this hyperactivity, allowing the prefrontal cortex (responsible for reasoning and decision-making) to regain control. This balance is critical for emotional health.

• A study by Dr. James Pennebaker found that writing about emotions, particularly traumatic experiences, significantly improves mental health. His "expressive writing" research shows that acknowledging and processing emotions reduces stress and boosts immune function.

The Role of Emotions in Manifestation

Neuroscience has revealed fascinating insights into this interplay. Studies on emotional resonance demonstrate that emotions activate parts of the brain linked to goal-oriented behavior, such as the prefrontal cortex. Yet here's the kicker—this activation only happens when there's emotional intensity. Without emotion, the brain simply

processes the world as raw data, detached and lifeless.
Take a moment to think about this: the brain, for all its complexity, only needs oxygen, food, and water to survive. That's it. It doesn't care about your grand dreams or your beautiful home. Those things hold no intrinsic value for the brain's survival programming. But your emotions? They care deeply. They give life to these dreams, infusing them with meaning and urgency.

A Story of Emotional Power

Let me share a story:

There was once an athlete—let's call her Emma. She had a dream to win gold at the Olympics, but her early career was riddled with setbacks. Injuries plagued her, and for a while, she considered quitting altogether.

She sought advice from her coach, who told her something that changed her perspective forever:

"Emma," he said, "your body doesn't care about gold medals. It doesn't even care about winning. But your heart does. You need to remember why you want this—not because of the medal, but because of the joy it brings you to run, the pride you feel in becoming your best self. When you focus on that, the body will follow."

It wasn't strategy or logic that carried Emma to the Olympic podium. It was the fire of her emotions—the pride, the joy, and the fierce determination she connected to her vision.

Why This Matters to You

Emotions are the true architects of your motivation. They don't just move you forward; they are the bridge between where you are now and where you dream of being. They are why you wake up early to work on a passion project, why you fight for your dreams even when the odds seem stacked against you.

So, when you hear someone say, "You're too emotional," what they are really saying—without realizing it—is, "You feel too deeply. You care too much." But ask yourself this: isn't feeling deeply and caring passionately the very essence of life?

Imagine removing those emotions. Sure, you might avoid the sting of disappointment or heartbreak, but at what cost? You'd also lose the euphoria of joy, the thrill of success, and the profound satisfaction of living a life aligned with your heart's truest desires.

Motivation doesn't reside in the brain. It resides in the fire of your emotions. Let that fire burn brightly, for it is your greatest ally in creating the life you are destined to live.

The Tea Cup and the Storm

A young monk approached his master, his heart weighed down by anger and frustration. He bowed deeply and confessed, "Master, my emotions are like a storm. They rage uncontrollably. Sometimes I feel anger so intense it consumes me, and other times sorrow so deep it drowns me. How can I silence them?”

The master, calm as the still waters of a mountain lake, said nothing. Instead, he rose and beckoned the young monk to follow him. They walked in silence to the meditation garden, where the master placed a small, delicate teacup on a large, flat stone. The cup was empty.

“Sit and observe,” the master said simply.

The monk, though puzzled, obeyed. For hours, they sat in silence as the winds rose and a storm began to brew. Dark clouds rolled in, and soon the skies unleashed their fury. Rain poured down relentlessly, and the wind howled through the trees. The teacup, fragile and exposed, shook but did not shatter.

When the storm subsided, the master stood and walked over to the teacup. Water filled it to the brim, but it remained intact. He lifted it and handed it to the monk.

“Your emotions are like the storm,” the master said gently. “They come and go, often wild and unrelenting. But you—your true self—are the teacup. No matter how fierce the storm, you remain unbroken. Your task is not to silence the storm but to strengthen the cup.”

The young monk gazed at the cup, the water reflecting the clearing sky above. For the first time, he understood. His emotions were not enemies to be fought but visitors to be acknowledged, allowed, and eventually released. It wasn’t the storm he needed to control but the steadiness of his own being.

Chapter Five

The Chaos of Desire

Even psychology acknowledges this phenomenon, referring to it as the "chaos of emotions." Often, it starts with desire—an intense wanting that spirals out of control, like a fire consuming everything in its path. It begins with a shock, but soon emotions like anger, fear, panic, sadness, and eventually despair take over. Your mind becomes a battlefield, with each emotion fighting for dominance, leaving you utterly exhausted and drained.

Grief follows a similar path. Imagine losing someone you deeply love, and after a year or two, you think you've come to terms with the loss. Then, suddenly, like a dormant volcano erupting without warning, grief strikes again. The shock returns, and the world around you, which has long moved on, fails to understand the chaos that has resurfaced within you.

This emotional chaos often leads to confusion. The people around you might not know how to help, or they may assume something is fundamentally wrong, suggesting you see a therapist or psychiatrist. Yet, the truth is, it's simply the natural way the human emotional system processes such intense feelings.

Emotions as Energetic Waves

Emotions are like waves of energy coursing through your body. Picture a still pond: one small stone—a single emotion—drops into the water, and ripples form. The ripples grow, colliding with others, and soon, what began as a subtle shift turns into churning waters. Sometimes, emotions stir quietly, like a breeze rustling the surface of a lake. Other times, they resemble a nuclear explosion, sending shockwaves through every layer of your being, shaking the very ground beneath you.

Just like the lingering radiation of an atomic blast, the effects of emotional chaos can endure long after the initial explosion. The intensity of these emotions may last for months or even years, quietly influencing your thoughts, decisions, and relationships. The key is learning how to isolate the core emotion—the source of the blast—and work with it. Otherwise, the emotional waves will continue to crash over you, pulling you under again and again.

The Trap of Multilayered Emotions

Emotional chaos rarely involves just one feeling at a time—it's the layers of emotions stacking on top of each other, like a tangled web. Let's say you're angry. At first, it's just that—a single emotion. But then guilt seeps in, as you start blaming yourself for feeling angry. Before long, sadness joins the mix, spiraling that initial emotion into a cascade of conflicting feelings. What began as a flicker has now grown into something that overwhelms, touching every corner of your inner world.

Chapter Five

The Chaos of Desire

Even psychology acknowledges this phenomenon, referring to it as the "chaos of emotions." Often, it starts with desire—an intense wanting that spirals out of control, like a fire consuming everything in its path. It begins with a shock, but soon emotions like anger, fear, panic, sadness, and eventually despair take over. Your mind becomes a battlefield, with each emotion fighting for dominance, leaving you utterly exhausted and drained.

Grief follows a similar path. Imagine losing someone you deeply love, and after a year or two, you think you've come to terms with the loss. Then, suddenly, like a dormant volcano erupting without warning, grief strikes again. The shock returns, and the world around you, which has long moved on, fails to understand the chaos that has resurfaced within you.

This emotional chaos often leads to confusion. The people around you might not know how to help, or they may assume something is fundamentally wrong, suggesting you see a therapist or psychiatrist. Yet, the truth is, it's simply the natural way the human emotional system processes such intense feelings.

Emotions as Energetic Waves

Emotions are like waves of energy coursing through your body. Picture a still pond: one small stone—a single emotion—drops into the water, and ripples form. The ripples grow, colliding with others, and soon, what began as a subtle shift turns into churning waters. Sometimes, emotions stir quietly, like a breeze rustling the surface of a lake. Other times, they resemble a nuclear explosion, sending shockwaves through every layer of your being, shaking the very ground beneath you.

Just like the lingering radiation of an atomic blast, the effects of emotional chaos can endure long after the initial explosion. The intensity of these emotions may last for months or even years, quietly influencing your thoughts, decisions, and relationships. The key is learning how to isolate the core emotion—the source of the blast—and work with it. Otherwise, the emotional waves will continue to crash over you, pulling you under again and again.

The Trap of Multilayered Emotions

Emotional chaos rarely involves just one feeling at a time—it's the layers of emotions stacking on top of each other, like a tangled web. Let's say you're angry. At first, it's just that—a single emotion. But then guilt seeps in, as you start blaming yourself for feeling angry. Before long, sadness joins the mix, spiraling that initial emotion into a cascade of conflicting feelings. What began as a flicker has now grown into something that overwhelms, touching every corner of your inner world.

These layers of emotion can tear apart relationships, too. Anger by itself may not destroy a bond, but when it's combined with guilt, resentment, and unspoken words, even the strongest connections can begin to crumble. If you don't learn to address the initial emotion, it will snowball into something much larger—disrupting not only your relationships but also your health, creativity, and sense of self.

The Art of Isolation

So, how do you combat this emotional intensity? By learning to isolate the primary emotion. When everything feels overwhelming, the first step is to find the source. What is the true root of your emotional overwhelm? Is it fear? Anger? Grief? Once you can pinpoint the core emotion, you can begin to work with it, rather than letting the surrounding confusion take over.

For instance, imagine you're angry with someone close to you—perhaps a partner, a friend, or a family member. Instead of letting the anger fester and attract guilt or resentment, you step back and identify it: "I'm angry because..." You acknowledge the emotion, express it, and begin to move forward. In that moment, the chaos starts to dissolve. You've cut off the source before other emotions can latch on and make things more complicated.

This approach is not just a tool for managing emotions—it's a way of life. Relationships, especially, are where emotional chaos often plays out most intensely, but by learning to isolate and work with a single emotion at a time, you can prevent these emotional storms from destroying the connections you value most.

The Power of Emotional Intelligence

Your brain, much like an advanced computer, is capable of processing vast amounts of information. But when emotions pour in like a downpour on parched ground, your brain begins to struggle. It shifts into survival mode, desperately seeking external solutions to restore a sense of stability. You might find yourself overthinking, compulsively checking messages, or seeking constant reassurance from friends. Yet, this illusion of control often does the opposite—it pulls you deeper into the cycle of overwhelm.

True mastery comes from within. It's not about controlling emotions but understanding them. Emotions aren't enemies to be battled—they are guides, pointing you toward deeper truths about yourself. They are signposts on the road to self-awareness, leading you through the fog of uncertainty. When you understand why you're angry, afraid, or grieving, those emotions lose their power over you. They transform from chaotic waves into gentle currents, guiding you safely through life's challenges.

This is where spiritual wisdom becomes invaluable. Emotions are messengers from the soul, carrying information about what's happening within you and around you. While the brain might try to solve everything logically, emotions speak a different language—one that is subtle, nuanced, and deeply connected to the spiritual realms.

They are not meant to be "fixed" but rather felt, understood, and integrated into your being.

Embrace the Human Experience

You were not placed on this Earth to avoid emotions or diminish their power. You are here to move through them, to grow with them, and to experience the vast, beautiful spectrum of what it means to be alive. Just as a river carves its way through stone, shaping the landscape over time, you too can allow emotions to flow through you without losing your foundation. By embracing this process and working with each emotion as it arises, you uncover the stillness within the noise.

You were not created to be flawless; you were created to be real. And within your authenticity lies the profound ability to transform every emotional wave into a chance to connect more deeply—with yourself, with others, and with the infinite wisdom of the universe. In this transformation, you become the anchor in the current—grounded, resilient, and a source of strength for those who find themselves adrift in their own emotional journeys.

Chapter Six

The Emotional Spectrum: Measuring Intensity

Let me present to you a scale of emotional intensity—a fascinating perspective rooted not in spiritual teachings but in psychology.

Yes, psychology, the realm of empirical studies and scientific validation. But here's the twist: even in this official psychological framework, energy reigns supreme.

That's right—at the top of the pyramid of emotional health and stability lies energy and survival. And no, I didn't sneak this in. It's a recognized, official concept in psychological circles. How remarkable is that? Psychiatrists and psychologists, though often distant from spirituality and energy work, openly acknowledge this truth.

Why, you might ask? Because science backs it up.

This scale, designed to map human emotional stability, reveals what we truly need most at our core:

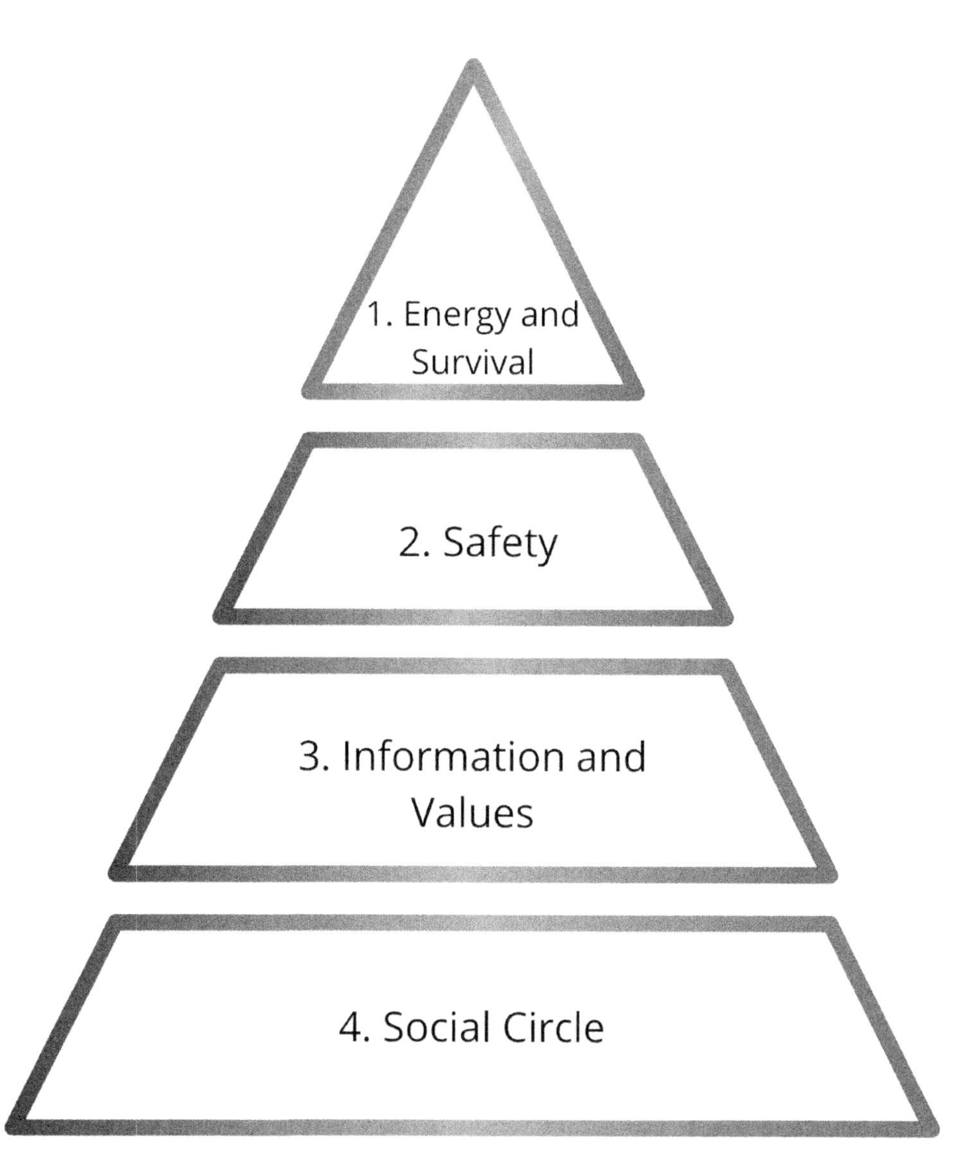
1. Energy and
Survival
2. Safety
3. Information and
Values
4. Social Circle

1. Energy and Survival

At the pinnacle of emotional stability is the fundamental need for energy—the driving force that enables us to act, move, and thrive. Imagine a person so utterly depleted of energy that they cannot even lift their arm or take another step. It's terrifying, isn't it? Without energy, survival feels impossible.

While psychology may frame "energy" in terms of biological resources—atoms, molecules, and physical vitality—those of us who understand the deeper layers know this includes spiritual energy as well. Without energy, everything stops.

2. A Sense of Safety

Next on the scale is the profound human need for safety. This means different things to different people. For some, it's the assurance of physical safety—living in a place free from crime or danger. For others, it's the knowledge that someone has their back, providing a sense of emotional and psychological security. Safety is the foundation upon which trust and stability are built.

3. Information and Values

The third level addresses information and values. Clarity about our circumstances and alignment with our personal values are critical for emotional balance. When people feel lost or unsure of their principles, their emotional health suffers. This layer ties deeply into our decision-making, purpose, and ability to process the world.

4. Social Connections

Surprisingly, relationships and social circles come only at the fourth level. While human connection is undeniably important, it ranks lower than energy, safety, and clarity. Social bonds are enriching, but without the foundational elements above, they can falter.

Exercise:

When an intense emotion arises:

- Identify its position on the scale.

- If it ranks high (e.g., impacting energy or safety), your emotional stability could be under significant threat.

- Act quickly to address it and prioritize your well-being based on where the need lies on the scale.

This approach helps you understand your emotional triggers and take actionable steps to regain balance.

.

Let me paint a scenario:

Even if you deeply love someone, truly love them with all your heart, if that person were to attack you in the middle of the night with a weapon, your instinct wouldn't be to stay—it would be to protect yourself. You'd leave, no matter how much you loved them. Why? Because safety and survival are at the top of the hierarchy.

People often say, "I'm emotionally shattered because this person meant everything to me." But let's unravel that thought. Is it really true? Or is it a story we weave around the emotions we feel for others? No one—not even the most cherished soul in your life—is truly irreplaceable. Even the idea of twin flames or soulmates is romantic, but not singular. The soul knows this. It recognizes there isn't just "one" person out there.

This doesn't make your emotions any less real, but it reminds us that our attachments often carry myths and expectations that magnify the drama and pain we feel.

At the core of it all, you must prioritize yourself.

Think about it—if you truly loved someone, wouldn't their well-being matter more than being with you? Why do we attach the condition that love must equal togetherness? Why do we insist on having someone physically present to validate our emotions?

The truth is, love isn't what breaks us. It's the emotional constructs we build around relationships—the stories we tell ourselves about what should be.

This is where understanding the Scale of Intensity becomes crucial. When a strong emotion hits, you need to evaluate its position on the scale. Is it draining your energy like a dried-up well on a scorching summer day?

If so, stop immediately and address it. But if the emotion is rooted lower on the scale—like a passing frustration with a colleague, or a minor disagreement in your social circle—you're not in immediate danger.

For example, let's say your boss had a bad day and took it out on you. It stings, but you know your partner at home loves and supports you, and you have the security of knowing your job isn't at risk. In this case, your emotional system may wobble but won't collapse.

However, if the event taps into something deeper—like draining your core energy or threatening your sense of safety—then it's a red flag. It's time to stop, regroup, and heal.

The scale teaches you how to navigate emotions with clarity. It helps you distinguish between passing challenges and deeper issues that need immediate attention. Recognizing this hierarchy allows you to stay grounded, even in moments of emotional upheaval.
Understanding your own needs on this scale isn't just self-care—it's self-mastery.

Chapter Seven

Unmasking Emotional Myths: The Truth Behind What We Feel

Myth #1: I Must Always Feel "Right."

This myth has roots in the Law of Attraction, which many misunderstood. Teachings that emphasized avoiding negative thoughts at all costs led to an unnatural suppression of emotions. Modern society excels at suppressing emotions, encouraging people to avoid "wrong" feelings and, in doing so, bypass a survival mechanism that's essential for navigating life. When emotions are suppressed, your system tries to alert you by triggering negative situations and emotions. These are louder, more survival-driven signals designed to grab your attention and bring you back on course.

Myth #2: Showing Negative Emotions Makes Me Look Weak.

This couldn't be further from the truth. Research has shown that when someone expresses negative emotions, it often prompts others to reflect on their own feelings, not judge the individual expressing them. For instance, seeing someone cry might bring up one's own sadness, or witnessing anger may make one reflect on how they feel being on the receiving end of such energy. Emotions are mirrors, not accusations, and vulnerability often fosters connection, not weakness.

Myth #3: Feeling Negative Emotions Means I'm a Bad Person.

This is a dangerous misconception. In fact, intense negative emotions are often experienced by people on the cusp of major spiritual breakthroughs. These emotions signal what you truly desire or reject in life and are essential for identifying your soul's purpose. Negative emotions often ignite survival instincts, fostering a sense of clarity and decisiveness. When understood, they can channel intense energy toward manifestation and transformation, rather than destruction.

Myth #4: Negative Emotions Are Destructive.

Not at all. Negative emotions are simply information. They deliver messages about what needs attention. However, when we ignore these messages, we risk becoming emotionally numb, like robots, and these unresolved emotions manifest in destructive behaviors: self-sabotage, overeating, isolating ourselves, or even turning to harmful substances. In severe cases, the soul intervenes, often through life lessons or emotional breakdowns, to reset and reawaken the original emotional system—survival. These moments of crisis hold immense potential for rebuilding and restoring balance.

Myth #5: Some Emotions Are Pointless or Unnecessary.

This is entirely untrue. Every emotion, no matter how trivial it seems, carries meaning. For instance, feeling anger at someone driving too slowly may point to deeper issues, such as the stress of being overburdened or running out of time.

Myth #6: People Can Easily See and Understand Others' Emotions.

People don't see emotions; they see behaviors resulting from those emotions. Many people wear emotional masks, projecting behaviors that hide their true feelings.

For example, someone feeling lonely might act arrogant or dismissive, pushing others away despite their deep yearning for connection. We often assume we understand others' emotions based on our perspective, but they are not us, and we are not them. Even psychics must tread carefully, as their personal biases can skew their reading of someone's emotional state.

Chapter Eight

The Fiery Power of Anger: A Call to Listen

Let's begin with one of the most primal emotions—anger. It's an emotion we all experience, yet one of the most misunderstood. When anger surfaces, it can feel overwhelming, even dangerous. It's not like the playful exaggeration of steam blowing from a cartoon character's ears; real anger is far more complex, far more powerful. It takes over in ways we don't always anticipate, often leaving us regretful for what we said or did in the heat of the moment.

I know this feeling all too well.

I'll never forget the day I almost did something unimaginable. Deep in grief over the loss of my mother, my emotions felt like a tidal wave—unrelenting, suffocating, pulling me under. I was consumed by a pain so profound that it blurred my sense of reality. Then my husband, grappling with his own way of coping, uttered words that shattered what little composure I had left: "It's not my fault your mom died. Life goes on for others."

Those words struck like lightning, igniting a firestorm of anger, sorrow, and disbelief within me. It was as though the weight of my grief had finally found a single, explosive point of release. In that moment, I felt lost, drowning in emotions too vast to control, teetering on the edge of my own limits.

It wasn't just a moment of frustration—my entire being was on fire. My head felt like it was boiling, and I could almost hear the rush of blood in my ears. Reality slipped away, and I lost all sense of who I was. The surge of hormones flooded my body, and I was no longer in control. The rational part of my mind shut down, leaving only raw emotion in its place. I was deeply, dangerously angry.

In that instant, I snapped.

I grabbed a knife. I was ready to lash out at the person I loved most because the pain I was feeling had taken over every part of me. I felt betrayed—by life, by everything—and I turned that fury onto him. Thank God I didn't go through with it. He stopped me, and I am forever grateful because I love him more than words can say. But it terrifies me to this day—I could have killed him.

Looking back, I see how far we've both come. He would never say something like that now; we've both grown, learned, and healed since that day. But the memory lingers, a reminder of just how powerful emotions can be when they spiral out of control. It's a moment I will never forget, and one that still frightens me when I think about how close I came to losing everything.

That kind of anger is so, so dangerous. It's not just a fleeting emotion—it's a force that can take over completely. And when it does, it's as though you're no longer yourself. The scariest part? It doesn't just appear out of nowhere—it builds up over time, fed by suppressed emotions, unspoken frustrations, and deeply ingrained patterns.

When we push our feelings down, when we don't express or deal with them in a healthy way, they don't vanish. They fester. They gather strength beneath the surface until one day, something small, something seemingly insignificant, triggers an explosion. That day with my husband wasn't just about his words—it was the culmination of years of suppressed grief, anger, and unresolved pain.

Anger like that grows from the inside, a slow burn that can suddenly ignite into a raging fire. And once it's unleashed, it's nearly impossible to control. That's why acknowledging and processing emotions as they arise is so crucial. When anger is left to simmer, it becomes a ticking time bomb—one that can destroy everything in its path if not defused in time.

But here's the thing: anger isn't inherently wrong. It's a messenger, albeit a loud and sometimes chaotic one. Anger shows up when something vital has been disrupted, when a boundary has been crossed, or when your soul's deepest values have been trampled. It demands your attention, and it demands it now.

The Boiling Point

When anger reaches its peak, as it did for me that day, there's no escaping its grip. Your body tenses, your heart races, and your mind spirals into chaos. In those moments, everything else vanishes—logic, reason, even the people around you. Anger takes over completely, like a fire blazing out of control, fueled by everything you've suppressed. It's as if all the emotions you've been bottling up collide at once, creating a force so powerful it feels like you might shatter under its weight.

I've seen this in myself, and I've seen it in others. When anger takes hold, it feels as if you've entered another world—one where nothing makes sense, and nothing feels safe. Your body floods with adrenaline and cortisol, and your emotions are no longer just feelings—they're physical sensations. Your chest tightens, your heart races, and your thoughts spiral out of control.

But here's something important: anger isn't your enemy. It's not something to fear or suppress. In fact, the more you suppress it, the stronger it becomes. It doesn't disappear just because you push it down. Instead, it simmers beneath the surface, waiting for the next opportunity to erupt.

Think of anger as a volcano. It can lie dormant for years, but eventually, the pressure builds, and when it erupts, it's unstoppable. The lava pours out, destroying everything in its path. But what if, instead of waiting for the explosion, you could release the pressure before it becomes destructive?

Anger as a Messenger

Anger isn't just a reaction—it's a signal. It's your body and mind's way of telling you something is wrong. It's trying to get your attention, like an alarm bell ringing in the middle of the night. If you ignore it, the sound only grows louder, more urgent.

When I felt that boiling anger rise in me, I didn't understand its message. I let it take control, and in doing so, I lost myself to it. But with time and reflection, I've come to see anger as a powerful guide. It shows up when something important is out of alignment—when your core values are being threatened, or when something crucial to your soul's purpose is being disrupted.

Anger often arises when something blocks your path to manifestation. You're moving along, creating, building, working toward something important, and suddenly, an obstacle appears. That obstacle—whether it's a person, a situation, or even your own doubts—triggers anger because it stands between you and your dreams.

And it's not just about the present—it's about time. Time is precious, and when something wastes your time, it feels as though it's stealing your most valuable resource.

Let's say you get angry because someone disrupted your plans. Instead of focusing on how awful it is that they did that, it's crucial to shift your mindset and start searching for constructive solutions that will help restore your original plan. If it's not possible to go back, you need to find something that will, within a reasonable timeframe, re-establish the essence of what you were working toward. Then, you affirm that and meditate on it using the "Gift Box of Emotions" meditation. You hold onto that vision as if it were your lifeline. Then, through both communication and action, you do everything necessary to bring back the energy that existed before the anger set in.

Anger will stay if you don't take this step. If you allow yourself to act in a way that feels wrong, or if the anger was triggered by someone else's actions, and thus feels foreign to you, it will linger. You need to restore what was disrupted before anger has the chance to settle in for good.

Or, let's say you get angry because someone told you that you won't succeed in your project. If you allow yourself to dwell on their criticism and let the anger fester, you're unconsciously reinforcing doubt in your project—or worse—allowing their opinion to infiltrate and influence it. And that's the last thing we want.

When you set boundaries, you're telling your subconscious, "This is what I will accept, and this is what I won't."

For example, if someone undermines your work, instead of stewing in anger, you calmly set a boundary:

"My journey is my own. Your opinion has no power here. I am reclaiming my path, and I won't allow you to interfere."

The Trap of Suppression

But here's the problem: most people don't know how to deal with anger. They suppress it, thinking that's the "right" thing to do. They push it down, ignore it, or tell themselves to "calm down." But that doesn't work.

Anger doesn't go away just because you pretend it's not there. Suppression is like putting a lid on a boiling pot—it might stop the steam for a moment, but eventually, the pressure will blow the lid off. I've seen this happen countless times, both in myself and others. People say, "I was so angry, but I calmed down."

But if you look closely, you can see that the anger didn't truly disappear. It was just buried, waiting for the next opportunity to surface.

True peace doesn't come from ignoring anger—it comes from acknowledging it. You must face it head-on, listen to what it's trying to tell you, and then release it in a healthy way. You can't jump from anger to calm without understanding the message behind the emotion. You have to ask yourself, "What is this anger really about?"

A Sacred Story: The Warrior and the Flame

In ancient teachings, there's a story about a warrior who once sought to control his anger. He lived in a village where honor and strength were prized above all else. The warrior, known for his fierce temper, often found himself in battles—not just with others, but with his own inner flame.

One day, after a particularly intense fight, the village elder called him aside. The elder was wise, a man of few words, but his presence was calming, like a river flowing through a dry desert. He asked the warrior, "Why do you fight the flame inside you?"

The warrior, confused, responded, “Because it burns too hot. It destroys everything around me.”

The elder smiled gently and said, “The flame is not your enemy. It is your guide. You fight it because you do not understand it. But what if, instead of fighting, you asked the flame what it wants to show you?” The warrior took the elder’s words to heart. The next time he felt the anger rise within him, instead of lashing out, he asked, “What do you want me to see?” And in that moment, the flame softened. It showed him the path he had been ignoring—the path that would lead him to peace.

Anger, like the flame, is not meant to be extinguished. It’s meant to illuminate the way forward. The key is not to fight it, but to understand it.

Next, we’ll dive into how to manage the emotion of guilt—another powerful force that can disrupt your inner peace.

.

Chapter Nine

Navigating Guilt: A Journey Through the Most Toxic of Emotions

Guilt is, without a doubt, one of the heaviest and most toxic emotions we can experience. It's not anger. It's not even rage, despite what some people might tell you. In fact, anger can be much healthier because it's often a release of energy, whereas guilt is deep, corrosive, and quietly destructive.

Guilt is toxic. It's a slow poison that seeps into your being and weighs you down. While true guilt, the kind that comes from genuinely hurting someone or going against your own moral compass, is rare, the guilt that most of us experience is learned.

True guilt? That might make up 10% of the guilt you feel. The rest of it—90%—comes from external sources. It's something you've been conditioned to feel. Society, culture, family, and even friends can impose guilt on you, manipulating your behavior, not just in the present but for the future as well. It's as if they're pulling your strings, turning you into their puppet. So, the first thing to understand is that genuine guilt is rare. The rest is often imposed upon you to control or influence you.

How Do You Deal With Guilt?

When you feel guilty, the first step is to ask yourself some important questions.

1. Do you agree with your actions?

For example, maybe you did something that you believed was right, but then someone else made you feel like it was wrong. Guilt sets in, and now you're questioning your own decisions. But, remove that person from the equation. Strip away their voice and focus only on your action.

Does it still feel right for your life and your path?

If the answer is yes, then that guilt doesn't belong to you. It's been projected onto you by someone else. You feel guilty not because of your actions, but because you're afraid of losing the relationship with that person, or you're afraid of judgment.

If you isolate the external influence and still feel like your actions were aligned with your values, then the guilt is misplaced. It doesn't belong to you.

2. When Anger Turns to Guilt

Sometimes, you might reflect on something you did in anger and feel guilty afterward. You might think, "I could have handled that better. I could've said it without raising my voice." But here's the thing—anger, as we've discussed, is often a tool. It's how your body or soul reacted at the time. Don't judge yourself harshly for it.

I've been in that space where guilt has followed after moments of anger. When I was furious—so furious that my head was boiling, and I felt I could have lost control completely—there were moments where guilt crept in afterward. Looking back, those were times when hormones overwhelmed me, and my sense of reality became blurred. I wasn't in control; the emotion was. But here's the truth: you have to forgive yourself for that.

If your actions align with your values, even if you were fiery in the moment, then guilt doesn't have a place. You were true to yourself. This is where the "Gift Box of Emotions" meditation comes in. Enter into this meditation and reaffirm your values. Tell yourself, "It's right that I think this way. It's right that I act this way, even if others don't understand it." If you don't do this, you risk becoming a puppet for others, moving to the strings they pull. And if you do that, your soul will feel the weight.

Staying True to Yourself

If your actions were in alignment with your nature, you need to reaffirm that. The guilt isn't yours to carry. It belongs to those who tried to impose their way of thinking onto you. If someone tells you, "You could have said that more gently," but you're naturally a fiery person, then you have two choices: you either suppress your natural energy and become what they want you to be, or you stay true to yourself and ask them to adjust to your energy.

Think about it—if you change to fit someone else's mold, it still won't be right. Eventually, they'll find something else to criticize. "You've changed so much, but I don't feel the spark from you anymore." You can't win by trying to satisfy everyone.

So, the real question is: Are you going to suppress your true self, or are you going to stay true to who you are?

When Guilt is Genuine: My Story

Now, let's say you did something that truly goes against your values—something that caused real harm. In this case, guilt has a purpose. You feel it because you need to make amends, to restore balance. When this happens, you simply apologize—to yourself first, and then to the other person.

But sometimes, guilt arises even when we logically know we shouldn't be responsible. That's the tricky part about grief and guilt—they often intertwine, leading us down a dark path of questioning and self-blame. This happened to me after my mother died of cancer.

When my mom passed away, I was overwhelmed with guilt. How could I be responsible? She had cancer, something beyond my control. And yet, I found myself spiraling into guilt, feeling like I hadn't done enough. I blamed myself for not being more observant of her health, for not pushing doctors harder, for not somehow seeing the signs earlier.

That guilt nearly crushed me.

It felt like I had failed in the most fundamental way—like I had let my own mother down. After she passed, that guilt didn't fade away; it grew. I carried it everywhere, as though my heart were chained to this immense weight. It took me to the very edge, mentally and emotionally.

But the truth is, no matter how much I obsessed over it, I couldn't have saved her.

The guilt I carried wasn't real—it was a reflection of my grief, a manifestation of the love I had for her, twisted into self-blame. The mind plays tricks on us during times of deep loss, making us believe we are somehow at fault for the inevitable. It wasn't until I deeply meditated on this, through tools like the "Gift Box of Emotions," that I began to see the truth.

I realized that my guilt was misplaced. It didn't belong to me. Yes, I loved her deeply, and yes, I would have done anything for her. But the cancer was beyond anyone's control. No amount of vigilance or questioning would have changed her fate.

Releasing the Weight

That's the wisdom you need to carry with you today. Guilt is a heavy stone that only grows heavier the longer you carry it. Whether it's guilt over your own actions or guilt imposed by others, you have the power to release it. Through reflection, meditation, and sincere apology (even to yourself), you can free yourself from the weight of guilt.

Old Teachings: The Burden of Unresolved Guilt

In ancient spiritual teachings, guilt was often seen as a weight that could drag a person down into a cycle of suffering. The Zen masters taught that unresolved guilt was like carrying a stone in your heart—every step you took, the stone grew heavier until it crushed the spirit.

There's an old Zen story about a disciple who confessed his guilt to his master. He had spoken harshly to a friend, and the guilt was weighing on him. The master, rather than offering advice, handed the disciple a large stone and asked him to carry it with him wherever he went. Days later, the disciple returned, exhausted and burdened, asking the master to take the stone away.

The master smiled and said, "The stone is your guilt. Only you can choose to set it down." In that moment, the disciple realized that the guilt he carried was self-imposed, and he was free to let it go.

Remember, your soul is too precious to be burdened by guilt that doesn't belong to you. Listen to your inner wisdom, reaffirm your values, and release anything that isn't in alignment with who you truly are.

That's how you walk the path of freedom from guilt.

Chapter Ten

What About Sadness?

Sadness appears when you think you're about to lose something, when you fear that something precious is slipping through your grasp. It feels like sand slowly falling through your fingers, and the harder you try to hold onto it, the more it escapes.

When you believe something dear to you is fading away, sadness creeps in like a cold mist, wrapping itself around your heart. Or perhaps, in some cases, you truly are losing something, something that meant the world to you.

But here's the thing—in 80% of cases, it's not real. It's merely a prediction, a whisper of fear, a thought that haunts your mind: "What if I lose this? What if it's no longer mine?"

This often stems from memories, echoes of the past when you did lose something, and now those memories trail behind you like shadows, casting doubt on your present. Sadness, in most cases, is that soft, anxious murmur: "What if? What if I lose this too?"

And more often than not, it's just a story—a film you play in your mind. A projection of your deepest fears.

That's when sadness turns on, like a dim light in a shadowy room, not fully illuminating but enough to create unease.

But here's something vital—80% of the time, you won't lose what you fear. The statistics show that when you brace yourself for loss, when you ready your heart for the pain, it's usually just a movie playing in your head. A fiction. Your mind conjures this film, based on fear or past hurts, making you think the worst is imminent.

The sadness that follows from these imaginings is unnecessary, a ghost of an emotion haunting something that hasn't even happened. And the good news? It's entirely solvable, quickly soothed through the magic of the "Gift Box of Emotions" meditation.

Now, in the 20% of cases where the loss is real—when you truly are facing the end of something precious, when a loved one is in their final days, and you know time is running out—then yes, sadness is inevitable. It fills your heart, knowing the days are numbered, knowing the end is near.

But if you find yourself in that 80% zone, where it's just the fear of loss, the solution is simple. Go into the "Gift Box of Emotions," open the magical chest, and see what's still yours. Take a moment to look at it—whatever it is you're afraid of losing. It's still there. It hasn't gone anywhere.

Such a simple solution, but it works like magic.

And if something truly is slipping away? If the end really is nearing, and there's nothing you can do to stop it? Then go into that "Gift Box of Emotions" again, but this time, pull out the love.

The deep love you have for that person, for that moment, for whatever it is that's fading away. Let that love cradle your sadness.

In this meditation, the love you find will hold your sadness like a tender promise. It will whisper to you: "I am here. Everything will be alright. You are not alone."

Sadness and love are like dance partners in life's grand ballroom. Where guilt and sadness can feel harsh and suffocating, sadness and love—ah, that's where the healing begins. It's a softer, more gentle release.

When I've faced real sadness, not just imagined fears, but the true loss of a loved one, a pet, or something deeply cherished, I had to dig deep. I had to pull out the most profound love I could find, and when I did, I always called upon the angels to guide me through.

And they held me. They held the person I was losing, the pet, the moment—whatever it was. In their embrace, I found peace. I learned that it's okay to let go, that love remains, even when everything else fades.

You can do this in the "Gift Box of Emotions." But sometimes, you might want to use the "Breathing Colors" meditation—we'll see which one resonates with you more. Both are beautiful, but each one holds a different energy. One takes you into a painting studio, filled with colors and creativity, while the other leads you into a toy shop of wonders and peace.

This is how you work with sadness.

And sometimes, it's just fear, isn't it? Fear that your husband will leave you, fear of losing something you hold dear. But that fear is just your imagination running wild, pulling from the past, comparing it to the present. Maybe someone hurt you once, walked out of your life, and now you expect the same thing to happen again.

But who says this person will do the same?

You're afraid, and because of that fear, you fall into sadness. But it's all based on comparing this moment to something from the past. The situations aren't even the same. It's a waste of your beautiful energy to dip into sadness over something that hasn't even happened. It's not helping you manifest anything good. In fact, that kind of sadness is unnecessary.
So, what do you do? You go into the "Gift Box of Emotions," and you pull out the truth. The truth that this person is still here. They haven't left you. They're still with you. Anchor yourself in that truth.

Sadness, you see, isn't stubborn.

Sadness likes to be comforted. It likes to be soothed. When you offer it love and warmth, it softens. It willingly accepts the love you give, and once you do, it's easier to work through.

Most importantly, remember this: 80% of the time, the sadness you feel is over something that might happen, but likely won't.

And yes, maybe 20% of the time, it's real. But why spend your precious energy being sad over something that hasn't happened yet?

It's like manifesting your own suffering. Why spend 80% of your time trapped in sorrow over something that's not even real?

Why would you want to do that? There's no sense in it.

Yes! There are several beautiful and profound stories and legends from various spiritual traditions that can deeply enhance the themes of sadness and emotional healing. Here's one that aligns perfectly with the themes of loss, love, and the healing power of perspective.

The Legend of the Broken Heart

In ancient Japan, there is a story about a famous potter named Hoshino. He was renowned throughout the land for creating the most exquisite pottery—delicate, flawless, and perfectly symmetrical. People from distant villages would travel for days just to buy one of his pieces, believing that they carried a special energy.

One day, Hoshino was working on a new commission, a beautiful bowl meant for the emperor himself. As he carefully spun the clay and shaped the delicate curves, disaster struck. A sudden noise startled him, and the bowl slipped from his hands, shattering on the floor into several large pieces.
Devastated, Hoshino sank to the ground. He wept over the loss of his creation and, more than that, over the dishonor of failing in such an

important task. His heart felt as though it had shattered alongside the bowl.

For days, Hoshino could not bring himself to enter his workshop. The broken pieces of the bowl still lay scattered across the floor, and he couldn't face them. It was not just the bowl that was broken—it felt like everything he was, everything he valued, was in pieces.
Then one evening, an old friend came to visit Hoshino. This friend was a wise man, known for his deep understanding of life and its trials. He found Hoshino sitting in darkness, his heart heavy with sadness.

"Hoshino," the wise man said gently, "Why do you grieve so deeply over the broken bowl?"

"Because it was perfect," Hoshino replied, his voice filled with sorrow. "And now it is destroyed. My work, my honor, everything is gone."

The wise man smiled softly. "But who says that perfection must be without flaws? Who says the cracks cannot become part of the beauty?"

Hoshino looked at him in confusion, and the wise man continued, "There is an ancient practice called "kintsugi", the art of repairing broken pottery with gold. The cracks, rather than being something to hide, become something to highlight. The bowl, once broken, is now even more beautiful, for its scars tell a story of resilience and transformation.

The gold illuminates the cracks, reminding us that what is broken can be healed, and that in healing, it becomes stronger and more radiant."

Hoshino was struck by the wisdom of his friend's words. The next day, he carefully gathered the broken pieces of the bowl and began the process of repair, using the finest gold to bind the fragments together. When the bowl was finished, it was more beautiful than before—its golden seams glimmered in the light, and its once-hidden fractures became symbols of rebirth.

The emperor, when he received the bowl, was moved to tears by its beauty. He understood that its value lay not in its original perfection, but in the story of its breaking and mending.

The legend of "kintsugi" teaches us that there is no shame in the cracks we carry, whether emotional or physical. Sadness, loss, and grief are like the cracks in Hoshino's bowl, but with time and love, they can be healed—transformed into something golden.

The process of healing makes us stronger, more beautiful, and more connected to the essence of life itself.

Our wounds, just like the golden seams, tell a story of resilience, and they make us shine in ways we never imagined.

The Lotus and the Mud

Another story often used in spiritual teachings comes from the tradition of Buddhism and Taoism. It's the story of the lotus flower and its journey from mud to beauty, symbolizing how sadness, hardship, and emotional turmoil can be the fertile ground from which love, compassion, and understanding bloom.

In a quiet, peaceful village nestled near a serene lake, lived a young boy named Tao. Each morning, he would walk by the water's edge, watching the graceful lotus flowers rise from the surface, their white petals glowing in the early morning sun. He marveled at their beauty, how they seemed so pure, so untouched by the world around them.

One day, Tao asked his grandfather, "Grandfather, how can something so beautiful grow in this muddy water?"

His grandfather smiled and led Tao to the edge of the lake.

"The lotus," he began, "is one of the most extraordinary flowers because of where it grows. You see the mud beneath the water? That mud is thick and dirty, full of decay and darkness. But it's from that very mud that the lotus draws its strength. The roots of the lotus dig deep into the muck, and from that muck, it finds the nourishment it needs to bloom so purely."

Tao looked down at the water and saw that, indeed, the mud was dark and thick, nothing like the pristine flowers floating above. "So the mud isn't bad?" Tao asked, confused.

"No," his grandfather replied gently. "The mud isn't bad at all. It is necessary. Without the mud, the lotus would never bloom. The beauty of the flower is not in spite of the mud, but because of it. And so it is with life, Tao. Our challenges, our sadness, and even our pain are the mud from which we grow. They are the fertile ground where we plant the seeds of compassion, wisdom, and love."

Tao's grandfather paused, then added, "When you face sadness, remember the lotus. Don't run from the mud of your life. Embrace it. Let it nourish you, and from it, you will bloom."

The lotus flower reminds us that the beauty of our souls often grows out of the most difficult and painful experiences. Sadness, like the mud, is not something to fear or avoid. It's the foundation from which growth, transformation, and wisdom emerge. Just as the lotus blooms pure and untainted from the dark water, so too can we rise from our sadness, transformed and radiant.

These legends align perfectly with your themes of sadness and emotional healing. The "kintsugi" story reflects the healing power of love, embracing brokenness, and transforming it into beauty, while the "lotus" teaches us that sadness and hardship are part of the path to personal blossoming and spiritual growth. Both stories remind us that our challenges, losses, and wounds are not the end, but the beginning of something even more profound and beautiful.

Chapter Eleven

Through the Veil of Fear: Transforming Panic into Peace

Fear and panic—two cunning visitors that often come uninvited. Many believe they are products of the mind, illusions conjured in moments of stress. But the truth runs much deeper. Fear and panic are born not from the mind, but from the emotional system, rooted deep within the heart and soul.

These emotions are often triggered by two forces. The first is past trauma—those moments of darkness that have left a shadow lingering in your heart, whispering, "What if it happens again?"

This is where fear gains its footing. Something familiar arises, and suddenly your mind races: "Could this be it? Could this disaster strike again?"

Of course, it's not the same. It never can be. But the emotional system, like a stubborn gatekeeper, locks onto that memory and matches it to the present, trying to force a key into a lock it was never meant for.
I know this all too well from my own experience. There was a time when any mention of cancer would send my heart spiraling into fear. Why? Because the only brush with cancer I had ever known was my mother's, and that story ended in death.

In my world, cancer equaled death. That was the narrative carved into my soul.

It was only after meeting people who had survived cancer, who had faced the illness and emerged on the other side, vibrant and alive, that I began to realize the truth. “Oh, cancer doesn’t always mean death.” But before that, the fear had taken root—so solid, so certain, even though it wasn’t the truth.

The second reason fear takes hold is much simpler: it is born from the unknown. There is nothing more unsettling for the emotional system than stepping into uncharted territory. When the path is unclear, when answers are out of reach, fear and panic rise like mist from the shadows.

So, what do we do when faced with these emotions? How do we find stillness amidst the inner unrest?

The answer lies not in suppressing the fear, nor simply “calming down.” Instead, we turn to a familiar ally—our magical meditation, “The Gift Box of Emotions”.

When fear grips you, when your mind is racing and your heart is trembling, you go to that box labeled “Fear.”

Now, inside this box lies the antidote to fear. If your fear stems from trauma, from something that happened in the past, you’ll pull out the opposite of fear—proof that your fear is unfounded.

Let me give you an example. I've known many mothers who fear the unimaginable—losing their child. It's a primal fear, one that grips the heart and refuses to let go. But the truth is, we cannot control the destiny of another soul, not even our own children. Their fate is intertwined with the divine. What we can control, however, is the energy we project into the world.

So, you open the box of fear, and what do you see? You see your child—alive, vibrant, and joyful, glowing like the sun. That's your reality, the truth of the present moment. The fear, the whispers that something terrible "might" happen, is a false story your mind has concocted.

That fear is not your truth

So, you let the image of your radiant child rise from the box like a warm, shimmering light. You see her laugh, dance, and create—this is the reality, not the imaginary disaster your mind tried to convince you of.

And yet, that sneaky voice might whisper again, "What about a year from now? What if..." Ah, that's where fear tries to trap you. But the future doesn't exist yet, not for you, not for anyone. It's a dream waiting to be shaped, and you have the power to craft it from love, not fear.

We don't manifest from fear. No. We create from hope, from trust, from the energy of "now".

Now, if fear and panic rise from the unknown, from uncharted paths where answers are scarce, the solution is simple. You seek information, you seek clarity. You go back to your "Gift Box of Emotions" and program into that box what you wish to manifest.

Instead of letting fear lead you down a path of doubt and paranoia, you learn to breathe through it.

Maybe you worry, "What if my partner leaves me?" and soon, you find yourself checking up on him constantly, seeking endless reassurance.

But that's not the way. Instead, go to the gift box, and pull out the image of your strong, loving relationship. See it, hold it close, and let "that" be your truth.

This is the gift you give yourself—this powerful, grounding truth.

And as we close, I will teach you a breathing technique—a special kind of breath that guides you back to peace, to the stillness within your heart.

This is how we face the waves of fear and panic. Not with resistance, but with love. Not with tension, but with trust. You have the tools, and now, you have the strength to bring peace to the turmoil within.

Gift Box of Emotions-meditation

- *Close your eyes. Let the world around you fade as you enter a space of calm and quiet.*

- *Allow yourself to completely relax, letting go of any tension in your body.*

- *Now, begin to journey into the realms of peace and tranquility.*

- *With each deep breath, inhale the soothing calmness of life. Feel the breath fill you with serenity.*

- *As you continue to breathe, imagine a soft, warm blanket gently wrapping itself around you.*

- *This blanket represents your sense of security, a warm cocoon that holds you in its embrace.*

- *It radiates warmth, light, and a deep sense of safety, calming your entire body.*

- *Breathe deeply, feeling the peace within the blanket's embrace.*

- *It's as if the entire universe is holding you, cradling you in this moment of perfect peace.*

- *Now, set your intention to step into the "Gift Shop of Emotions."*

• *You are about to create a beautiful manifestation, one that is born from positive emotions.*

•*Take a moment and ask yourself: What does your heart truly seek?*

• *Which emotion is calling you to step into this magical space?*

• *Perhaps it's an emotion that has been asking for your care—guiding you to the whimsical toy shop ahead.*

• *Do not fear this emotion; instead, embrace it.*

• *Just as it wraps itself around you, you offer it support in return.*

• *Now is the time to take the next step.*

• *Suddenly, a door appears before you—shining, inviting.*

• *Stand up and carry this moment of peace with you as you approach the door.*

• *Open the door, and step through into a world of wonder—a beautiful, enchanting toy shop.*

• *Sunlight pours in through large windows, illuminating plush bears, toys, colorful blocks, and endless wonders.*

• *This place speaks to your inner child—a sanctuary of magic and safety.*

- *Here, only goodness exists. You are completely safe.*

- *In one corner of this magical gift shop, you notice wooden blocks neatly stacked in vibrant colors.*

- *On each block, emotions are painted in delicate strokes, emotions you know so well.*

- *Approach these blocks and kneel beside them, feeling the warmth of this magical space.*

- *Look closely at the emotions depicted on these blocks—each one calls to you, asking for your care.*

- *Which emotion speaks to you in this moment? Which emotion is asking for your attention?*

- *Trust your intuition. Select your block and take it gently into your hands.*

- *When you are ready, open the block.*

- *From within, a shimmering hologram emerges, representing your positive manifestation.*

- *This is the outcome you desire from this very emotion—the beauty that is waiting to be born.*

- *It's a radiant vision, something you wish to transform, to create anew from this emotion.*

• *Offer this emotion peace, knowing that everything is truly okay.*

• *Hold onto this manifestation with great strength. Visualize it, feel it, speak it—express it however you wish.*

• *Understand that this is your reality. From this, new positive emotions are born.*

• *This is life's greatest gift—the power to create, transform, and grow.*

• *Let this blessing settle into your soul. Breathe deeply, knowing that this manifestation is yours.*

• *Feel the peace and security restored within you. Everything is truly alright.*

• *New emotions of deep peace and calm now live within you.*

• *You are ready to return to your life, carrying this harmony with you.*

• *As you count down from ten to one, feel yourself gently returning to the present moment, grounded and at peace.*

• *Ten. Nine. Eight. Seven. Six. Five. Four. Three. Two. One.*

• *You may now open your eyes, feeling safe and ready to embrace all the good that is unfolding in your life from this moment forward.*

Chapter Twelve

Breathing the Colors of Emotions: The Rhythm of Calm

Breathing—what a sacred role it plays in our lives. I've shared before how emotions seek a sense of safety, a refuge when everything else feels uncertain. And what better anchor than breath? When you breathe deeply, you feel safe. But take that breath away, even for a moment, and the sense of safety crumbles, as if the ground beneath your feet disappears.

Breathing is our tether, a conscious rhythm we can hold onto when all else feels chaotic. The beating of your heart may go unnoticed unless it pounds wildly, but your breath—ah, that is something you are always aware of. The rise and fall of your chest, the gentle flow of air—it's as if the very essence of life whispers through you with each inhale and exhale.

Emotions are deeply connected to this rhythm. They find solace in it, feel safe in its cadence. That's why we weave breathing into our meditations, especially when navigating the turbulent seas of emotions.

There are two meditations I've shared with you, both centered around this sacred breath. The first, "The Gift Box of Emotions", doesn't focus specifically on breath, but the second—ah, the second is crafted entirely for this purpose. It's called "Breathing the Colors of Emotions".

In this meditation, you choose the color of your emotions, the one that represents what you feel most intensely. With each breath, you breathe that color in, shaping your reality with its power.

Breathing exercises have been scientifically proven to reduce stress, lower cortisol levels, and enhance overall mental health. Research shows that focused breathing activates the parasympathetic nervous system, bringing your body into a state of calm and reducing the fight-or-flight response that fuels panic and anxiety. Studies conducted by the American Psychological Association suggest that just a few minutes of deep breathing can significantly lower heart rate, improve cognitive function, and promote emotional balance. The act of controlling your breath allows you to control your state of mind, bringing clarity and peace into moments that otherwise feel overwhelming.

For some, this physical act of breathing is transformative—a bridge from chaos to calm. For others, the mind alone can guide them there. Some have transcended the need for this, relying solely on their energy flow, their aura, to do the work. But if you find that you need this physical anchor, this deep breath, that's perfectly okay.

Let's explore how it works, shall we?

When anger rages like wildfire in your soul, it often appears as a vivid color. For some, it's red—the color of passion, power, and fury. But for others, red might not represent anger at all. Perhaps it's the color of motivation or love. You must listen to your own soul, feel which color your anger wears.

When you feel the flames of anger, breathe into your belly. Slow, deep breaths. Many people have been taught to calm anger by slowing the breath, but oh, how often that backfires. For some, slowing the breath when fury strikes only fans the flames further. Imagine trying to contain a wildfire with a gentle breeze—it doesn't work.

When anger roars, sometimes you need to release it fully before you can find peace. If you've already let your anger speak its truth, only then can you use breath to release the remnants. Place your hands on your solar plexus, where your power resides, and breathe. Feel the energy begin to settle, like ash after a storm. Inhale through the nose, exhale through the mouth. This is how you reclaim your calm.

But what of guilt?

Ah, guilt—the stubborn stain on the soul. It clings like a shadow, refusing to let go. For guilt, the breath is different. You breathe in through your nose, hold it for just a moment—long enough to feel it, but not long enough to be uncomfortable. Then, with a powerful exhale, you release. Let it go. Not gently, but with force, as though you are pushing the guilt out of your body.

Place one hand on your heart, the other on your belly, and feel the breath move between them. Don't hold your breath for too long—guilt doesn't need to be invited to stay. You listen to your body, and when the time is right, you let it go.

Now, sadness... sadness is a different kind of guest. It is quiet, soft, and tender. For sadness, the breath must be even, natural. In through the nose, out through the nose, with your hands resting over your heart—not just your chest, but over the very center of your heart.

Do you know what happens when your heart feels the warmth of your hands? It's like a gentle hug, a whisper of comfort. Imagine holding a small, fragile bird in your hands—that's the tenderness your heart feels when you breathe with this touch. Your heart softens, like a flower unfurling in the morning sun, and sadness, well, it wraps itself in the love you give and settles into peace.

And for fear, for panic—these require deeper, stronger breaths. You breathe into your belly, slow but powerful. If you can, breathe both in and out through your mouth, though if that feels too unsettling, adjust as needed.

Place your hands on your ribs, feel your body expand with each breath, grounding yourself in your own strength.

Fear tries to make you small, but this position, these deep breaths, remind you of your power. With each breath, you claim your space, your presence, your courage.

And remember, in all these practices, you are the master of your breath. Each emotion may call for a different rhythm, a different color, but ultimately, it is your breath that guides you.

Through anger, guilt, sadness, and fear, we navigate these waters with the same tool—the breath. In the "Breathing the Colors of Emotions" meditation, you will choose which emotion to work with, and with each breath, you will transform it. Whether it's reaffirming your values or simply acknowledging what is, you will find your center.

We have completed this step together, and now I leave you with the magic of your breath. Let it carry you through, let it calm the fires, and may it always bring you back to peace.

The Colors of Emotions: A Meditation for Inner Harmony

- *Find a comfortable position. Feel the weight of your body grounded.*

- *Gently close your eyes, letting the world around you soften.*

- *Begin to take deep, calming breaths, feeling the air fill your lungs and slowly release.*

- *As your breathing deepens, a wave of acceptance washes over you, like a gentle tide embracing the shore.*

- *Little by little, colorful dots begin to appear on your aura, shimmering like liquid light.*

- *These hues are vibrant and strange, swirling across your energy field, each representing a part of you—your emotions, thoughts, desires, and visions.*

- *You realize that, just as you cannot pick a single part of a painting as the most beautiful, you cannot pick a single part of yourself. Together, all these colors make you whole, and you embrace them fully.*

- *Take a moment to witness the colors of your being. Feel them blend, shift, and dance in harmony.*

- *Breathe in, accepting every emotion, every hue, every part of who you are.*

- *Now, honor what arises. Whether it's joy, sorrow, love, or anger—honor it. This is your true essence.*

- *Your natural energy expands outward, like rays of sunlight touching every corner of your being.*

- *Suddenly, a door appears before you—a doorway to a magical artist's studio, inviting you to step inside.*

- *Guided by curiosity, you open the door, feeling a sense of wonder as you step into the space.*

- *The room is filled with palettes and brushes, glowing with a beautiful energy. You feel an ancient, creative presence here.*

- *Your eyes are drawn to one particular palette. It seems to call out to you, holding the color of the emotion that most needs your attention.*

- *What emotion within you is seeking support right now?*

- *Pick up the palette with both hands. Feel its weight, its energy, and connect deeply with that emotion.*

- *Now, choose where you will place your hands—over your heart, your chest, your stomach, or your sides. Trust your instinct. As your hands find their place, breathe for this emotion. Breathe deeply, and let the color of this emotion fill your entire being.*

- *The emotion receives your love and attention. It is seen, acknowledged, and held in the light of your presence.*

- *These are the colors of your soul. With every inhale, breathe in acceptance. Feel the power in these emotions, the beauty that arises when they are embraced fully.*

- *Breathe in safety, knowing that this is how you touch the innermost part of yourself.*

- *Watch now as the color begins to dance, swirling from your palms, forming into pure energy before your eyes. This energy holds your deepest desire, the manifestation you've longed for.*

- *Suddenly, the color shifts, transforming into something radiant—perhaps a different hue entirely, something so full of love.*
- *The energy flies forward, landing on the canvas before you. On this canvas, your vision starts to take shape.*

- *What you desire, what your heart has wished for, now begins to shine—*

born from the emotions you honored, from the truth of your being.

- *Watch as this creation takes form. Perhaps it's love, perhaps peace—whatever your heart longs for is now manifesting before you.*

- *In this magical realm, here is the painting of your life—the painting of happiness, of peace, of fulfillment.*

- *As your vision is born on the canvas, new emotions arise within you—a deep sense of safety, a profound trust in the journey ahead.*

- *Become fully aware of this painting, this beautiful creation, and let it imprint itself in your soul. It is yours, and it will guide you forward.*

- *The colors of your emotions hold you now, tenderly cradling you in peace, love, or whatever feeling you most need.*

- *Now, it's time to bring this vision into your waking life. Trust that the colors on the palette will guide your journey ahead.*

- *As I count down, begin to return to the present, carrying this vision with you.*

- *Five. Four. Three. Two. One. You are fully present now, grounded in your body, feeling wonderful and light, back on Earth.*

- *Open your eyes and step into your new vision, ready to live what you have created.*

Part Three

Designing the Inner Sanctuary

Chapter Thirteen

The Body: Cornerstone of Inner Peace

Welcome to the third pillar of your journey, a blueprint for deeper understanding and harmony. In the earlier chapters of this expedition, we explored the intricate landscapes of emotions—anger, sadness, and guilt—unraveling the threads that tether us to their intensity. Each emotion we encountered was like a churning ocean, and we moved through it with courage, learning to navigate its waves and steer ourselves toward the calm waters of inner peace.

Now, we shift our focus to the physical foundation of this architecture: the body. At first glance, the connection between the body and inner peace might seem tenuous. After all, isn't it the mind and emotions that dictate our chaos and calm? Yet here lies a profound truth: the body is not merely a vessel; it is a sanctuary, a keeper of secrets, and a compass guiding us toward self-reclamation.

Imagine the body as the cornerstone of your inner peace—a sturdy structure that holds the weight of your experiences. When emotions rage like unrelenting winds, it is the body that bears their fury. The tightness in your chest during fear, the sinking sensation of guilt, the tension in your shoulders from anger—all these are whispers from the body, begging to be heard, seeking release.

To heal the emotional imbalances, we must return to the foundation itself. Emotions carve their presence into our physical being, manifesting as tightness, fatigue, or discomfort. Anger grips the jaw, sadness slows the rhythm of our movements, and guilt presses heavily on our shoulders. Ignoring the body in the pursuit of inner peace would be like attempting to compose a symphony without first tuning the instruments.

Science confirms what ancient wisdom has long understood. Research reveals that emotions trigger biochemical responses in the body, from stress hormones to tightened muscles, creating physical manifestations of emotional turmoil. Ancient practices, from yogic traditions to indigenous rituals, have always honored the body as a sacred partner in healing. And now, modern medicine echoes their truths: the mind and body are inextricably linked.

In this part of the journey, we will dive into the body's sacred language. Just as an architect learns to read blueprints, we will learn to interpret the body's messages. When the chest tightens, what is it telling you? When fatigue strikes, what unspoken burden is your body carrying? By answering these questions, we will build not only understanding but also a profound sense of calm.

This chapter will invite you to reconnect with your body as a friend and guide. Together, we'll explore how to release tension, restore energy, and foster a sanctuary within your physical self. We will look at simple yet transformative practices—mindful breathing, movement, and relaxation techniques—that allow the body to exhale the weight of unresolved emotions and inhale the essence of peace.

In the words of Rumi, "Don't ignore the call of your body. It is your guide to the treasure within." As architects of inner peace, we now turn to this sacred blueprint—the body—not to control or dominate it, but to listen, to honor, and to heal.

Here, within these pages, you'll find the tools to become the master builder of your own sanctuary, where your body and emotions coexist harmoniously. Let's begin the next phase of this construction, brick by brick, breath by breath. The architecture of inner calm awaits your touch.

The Symphony Between Mind, Body, and Immune System: Exploring Psychoneuroimmunology

Once upon a time, in a world where science and spirit walked separate paths, an idea emerged—one that would forever change the way we perceive ourselves. It was the revelation that the mind and body are not distant strangers, but star-crossed lovers, endlessly communicating through intricate whispers of biology and emotion. This union birthed a remarkable field of study: psychoneuroimmunology (PNI), the science that unravels the ancient dance between thoughts, feelings, and the immune system.

Much like the celestial mechanics guiding the orbits of planets, your body operates through a delicate balance of interconnected systems. The mind, the brain, the nervous system, and the immune system weave a complex tapestry that determines the quality of your health and well-being. What you think, what you feel, how you act—all echo through your body's physical realm, often in ways as profound as a ripple crossing a still pond.

The Birth of a Revelation

The roots of psychoneuroimmunology stretch back to the 1970s when the brilliant mind of Robert Ader, a pioneer in the field, illuminated what was once thought impossible: the brain and the immune system are in constant dialogue. Ader's discoveries tore down the walls that once divided psychology from immunology, revealing the mind as an architect of health or illness. He proved that stress—the silent thief of vitality—can weaken the immune system, just as joy can fortify it. Like a secret passage hidden in an ancient castle, PNI opened a door to understanding how emotions shape our immune defenses. Each thought becomes a note in the symphony of well-being, proving that no system in the body exists in isolation.

The Inner Mechanisms of the Mind-Body Connection

PNI unveils a profound truth: your body listens to your mind's whispers, whether they are gentle or chaotic. Let's imagine the process as a story of three acts:

1. The Storm is Born: Stress and the Nervous System
Picture this—a shadow passes over your horizon, and stress descends like a sudden tempest. Your hypothalamus, that ancient guardian of your brain, signals the adrenal glands to release cortisol, the "stress hormone."

This surge ignites the body's "fight or flight" response, preparing you to face the storm or flee from it.

2. The Messenger: Cortisol and Its Double-Edged Sword
Cortisol, though essential in short bursts, becomes the villain when the storm never ends. Chronic stress drowns the immune system, reducing antibody production and silencing T-cells—the brave knights that defend your body from invaders.

3. The Consequence: Immune Suppression
The immune system falters under the weight of prolonged stress, leaving the body vulnerable to infections, delayed healing, and even chronic illnesses.

Fascinating Glimpses into the World of PNI

1. Stress acts as both the hero and the villain. Acute stress can ignite the immune system, preparing it for battle. But chronic stress, like a slow-acting poison, erodes its defenses, leaving the body vulnerable to infections, slower healing, and even the shadow of diseases like cancer.

2. Depression whispers in the language of inflammation. It invites pro-inflammatory cytokines to take center stage, intertwining emotional suffering with physical decline, demonstrating how the mind's burdens can weigh heavily on the body.

3. The placebo effect, often dismissed as mere illusion, reveals the

brain's alchemical power. A simple belief in healing can rally the immune system's forces, proving that faith—whether in a pill or possibility—can alter the body's reality.

4. Laughter truly is medicine. It summons immunoglobulin A, the immune system's unsung hero, while banishing stress hormones like cortisol. Each laugh is a burst of endorphins, lighting the body's pathways with well-being.

5. Relationships are the immune system's secret allies. Bonds of love and connection fortify health, while loneliness sows the seeds of weakness. The warmth of companionship is not just a balm for the heart but a shield for the body.

6. Even in stress, there is duality. Acute stress, like a sprinter's burst of energy, can sharpen the immune response, while chronic stress, the marathoner's endless race, leads to its collapse.

7. During exam season, students become case studies in stress's toll. Levels of immunoglobulin A plummet, leaving them susceptible to illness—a vivid reminder of how the mind's pressures shape the body's defenses.

8. Sleep is the silent healer. In its embrace, the body produces cytokines, the architects of immune strength. When sleep is neglected, this restorative symphony falters, and immunity weakens.

9. The ancient practice of mindfulness finds modern validation. Meditation, yoga, and deep breathing restore balance, lowering cortisol and awakening the immune system's resilience.

10. Chronic diseases bear the fingerprints of prolonged stress. From autoimmune disorders to cardiovascular conditions, the mind's turmoil reverberates through the body, underscoring the importance of harmony within.

As we peer into the depths of PNI, the message is clear: the mind and body are not two separate kingdoms but a united empire. And within this empire, balance is the key to unlocking vitality and resilience. This leaves us with a question: How can we use this wisdom to transform our inner sanctuary? The answer lies ahead, waiting to be discovered.

We Are All "Lexie"

In 2015, a shattered life stumbled into my world—a nine-year-old rescue dog named Lexie. Her body bore the cruel map of her past, and her spirit was a tattered whisper of what it had once been. She had been beaten every day by her previous owners, her fragile frame absorbing years of unimaginable violence. The scars weren't just on her body; they ran deep within her soul, leaving her a shell of a being. Her body was a battlefield, her organs "glued together" by the trauma she had endured. The veterinarians spoke in hushed tones of her critical condition. Twelve surgeries in her first three years had barely kept her alive. Hematomas, shredded tissues, and failing organs painted a grim picture. They gave her a 5 to 10 percent chance of survival and gently suggested euthanasia. "Let her rest," they said.

But how could I? Looking into her eyes—eyes that carried the weight of every cruel blow, every moment of terror—I saw a flicker, a faint ember of life that refused to go out. Five percent wasn't nothing. It was something. And I decided, in that moment, that if she still had the courage to fight, so would I.

Lexie arrived at my home, but she didn't arrive in spirit. She lay motionless on the couch, her body barely functioning, her soul retreating into the darkest corners of despair. She didn't want to eat, walk, or engage with the world around her. The weight of her past hung over her like a shadow, and she had no reason to believe the light could ever break through again.

But love has a way of seeping into even the most shattered of hearts. It doesn't demand; it waits, gently chipping away at the walls of fear. Every day, I showed her kindness—a kind word, a gentle touch, a quiet reassurance that she was safe now. At first, she barely noticed. Her wounds were too deep, her trust too broken. But healing, as I would learn, is not an explosion—it is a quiet, persistent revolution.

By 2016, the first cracks of light began to appear. Her fur, once dull and brittle, began to soften. Her eyes, once clouded by sorrow, reflected the faintest glimmer of curiosity. She started to move, albeit cautiously, as though testing whether the ground beneath her feet would hold.

She even began to interact with my other dog, Tara, though their connection was tentative.

By 2018, Lexie was unrecognizable. Her coat gleamed with health, her eyes sparkled with life, and her steps carried a confidence that had once seemed impossible. The dog who had once been beaten into submission now ran with joy. She had claimed her place in the world, proving that no amount of darkness could extinguish her light.

The journey wasn't easy or inexpensive. Over 12,000 USD was spent on her surgeries—a sum that many deemed ridiculous for a dog. "Why spend so much?" they asked. But to me, the answer was clear. Lexie wasn't just a dog; she was a soul who had been robbed of everything good in life. She deserved more than survival; she deserved love, healing, and a chance to truly live.

Her transformation wasn't just physical. The revival of her spirit was nothing short of miraculous. Love, patience, and relentless belief in her potential became the medicine that healed her. It was as if every act of kindness helped piece her back together, one fragment at a time.

Today, Lexie is 18 years old, thriving beyond anyone's expectations. She has outlived Tara, my other beloved dog, who passed away at 17. Tara, who had been a "spoiled princess" from birth, never faced the horrors Lexie had endured. Yet it was Lexie, the warrior, who taught me the most profound lessons about resilience, forgiveness, and the boundless capacity of love to heal even the deepest wounds.

Lexie's story is a reflection of all of us. We are all Lexie, in some way—carrying scars, visible or hidden, from the battles we've faced. But her journey proves that no matter how broken we may feel, no matter how insurmountable the odds, there is a path to healing. With love, care, and unwavering belief, even the most shattered among us can rise—not just to survive, but to thrive.

The Body as a Mirror of the Mind

In the field of psychoneuroimmunology (PNI), the body is no longer seen as a passive shell but as an interconnected system, deeply entwined with our emotions and thoughts. Researchers have shown that the body doesn't just respond to the mind—it actively communicates with it. When stress, fear, or sadness flood the mind, the body absorbs this energy and translates it into physical sensations or symptoms. But the reverse is also true: the body can be a gateway to emotional calm, offering a path to heal the mind through intentional physical practices.

For example, studies have demonstrated that gentle touch can trigger the release of oxytocin, the so-called "love hormone," which reduces stress and fosters a sense of safety. Movement, such as yoga or even simple stretching, has been shown to balance the production of cortisol, the body's primary stress hormone. These findings affirm what ancient traditions have long understood: the body holds the power to heal not only itself but also the emotional unrest that often stirs within.

Chapter Fourteen

Techniques That Heal: Merging Science and Sensation

Some of the most transformative physical methods align with the principles of PNI, leveraging the body's innate wisdom to bring about emotional balance. Here are a few techniques backed by science:

• **Water as a Healer:** Hydrotherapy, or the use of water for therapeutic purposes, has been practiced for centuries and continues to gain recognition in modern medicine. Immersing oneself in warm water has been shown to lower blood pressure and reduce cortisol levels, creating a sense of profound relaxation. Cold-water immersion, on the other hand, can stimulate the vagus nerve, which plays a key role in calming the nervous system.

• **The Power of Visualization and Touch:** Combining visualization with touch can amplify the body's ability to heal. Studies reveal that imagining a warm, glowing light enveloping the body while practicing self-massage or gentle tapping can reduce anxiety and boost immune function. This dual approach bridges the gap between the conscious and subconscious mind, creating a dialogue that soothes both.

• **The Breath-Body Connection:** Breathing techniques are among the simplest yet most powerful tools for calming the body. Deep, diaphragmatic breathing slows the heart rate and signals the brain to shift from a state of stress to relaxation. Research shows that consistent practice can even alter neural pathways, making it easier to access calm in moments of distress.

- **The Grounding Effect of Nature:** Walking barefoot on grass, sand, or soil—known as "grounding" or "earthing"—has been scientifically proven to reduce inflammation and improve mood. The body's direct connection to the Earth's energy field can stabilize the nervous system and create a sense of inner peace.

The Body as a Storyteller

Each of these practices taps into the body's ability to tell its own story—a story of resilience, healing, and balance. The body remembers what the mind forgets, and through intentional practices, we can help it release what no longer serves us.

Imagine the body as a river, its currents shaped by the flow of emotions, thoughts, and experiences. When the waters are turbulent, they carve patterns that can become rigid over time. But with care, we can redirect these currents, allowing the river to flow smoothly once again.

As we learn to listen to the body's stories, we not only heal but also come to understand ourselves more deeply. The body, in its wisdom, shows us that the path to emotional calm is not separate from the physical—it is a partnership, a dance of two interconnected worlds.

Exercises of Body Stories: Cosmic Wave of Relaxation

- *Preparation: Stand under the shower or lie in the bath, creating a peaceful environment where you can focus without distractions.*

- *Visualize Connection: Imagine your body as a small ocean within a boundless cosmic ocean. See the water outside you merging with the water within your body, becoming one unified flow.*

- *Feel the Touch of Water: As water touches your skin, picture it filled with radiant light. Visualize this light-infused water entering your body and connecting with every cell.*

- *Release Tension: Imagine the waves of water and light dissolving tension, stress, and unease.*

- *Feel the flow washing through your muscles, releasing every knot of discomfort.*

- *Embrace the Cosmic Rhythm: Picture the water as a cosmic current, aligning your body with the rhythm of the universe.*

- *Allow the waves to calm your thoughts and replace heaviness with lightness.*
- *Finish with Gratitude: When you're done, mentally thank the water for its healing energy.*

- *Step out of the bath or shower with a sense of calm, harmony, and connection to the cosmos.*

Movement of Star Lines Exercise

Prepare Your Body:

- *Stand tall with feet hip-width apart and knees slightly bent.*
- *Close your eyes and take deep, slow breaths.*
- *Visualize your body surrounded by delicate threads of light—star lines stretching through the universe.*

Star Inhalation:

- *Slowly raise your arms above your head, drawing energy from invisible stars.*
- *Move your arms in wide, gentle circles, as though tracing light in the air.*
- *With each inhale, feel your connection to the cosmic energy surrounding you.*

Weave Star Lines:

- *Move your arms from side to side, softly weaving invisible star threads around your body.*
- *Visualize your movements creating a harmonious network of light.*
- *Let your movements flow intuitively, like a gentle dance.*

Create Star Waves:

- *Swing your arms forward and backward, forming waves of light.*
- *Slowly lift your arms above your head, then lower them in front of you.*
- *Feel your body merging with the smooth, flowing waves of star energy.*

Engage the Whole Body:

- *Bend your knees slightly and rotate your hips in slow circles, imagining your body drawing starry patterns in space.*
- *Stretch your arms in different directions, connecting your movements to the star lines.*
- *Feel your body becoming one with the cosmic energy around you.*

Release Emotional Blockages:

- *With every exhale, let go of tension and emotional blockages.*
- *Visualize trapped energies dissolving into the starry light, leaving your body free and flowing.*

Conclude the Exercise:

- *Gradually return to a standing position, arms relaxed at your sides.*
- *Take a deep breath and feel the cosmic energy flowing freely within you.*
- *Bask in the calmness and freedom of your realigned star lines.*

This practice not only grounds you but enhances your energy flow, aligning your body with the cosmic rhythm and accelerating manifestation.

Why Does It Work?

The Star Line Movement works by harmonizing the body, mind, and energy systems through a fusion of gentle movement and visualization. Inspired by the fluidity of tai chi and the grounding softness of yoga, this exercise activates your body's natural awareness, creating a pathway to release tension and emotional blockages.

The slow, deliberate movements combined with the imagery of weaving and aligning star lines invite your mind and body to collaborate, fostering a deep sense of relaxation and lightness. The visualization connects your physical being to the greater energetic universe, aligning your personal flow with a larger cosmic rhythm. This connection enhances the body's capacity to let go of stress and allows energy to flow freely, both physically and emotionally.

By becoming part of a symbolic "cosmic dance," you not only relax but also open pathways for emotional release and mental clarity, leading to a profound sense of calm and vitality. This integration of body and imagination taps into the subconscious, creating a symphony of movement and light that recharges your entire system.

It's not merely an exercise; it's an act of reuniting with the universe's natural flow—a reminder of the limitless energy that lies within and around you.

Sound Symphony of the Body

Using sound as a therapeutic ally, this exercise harnesses subtle tones and vibrations from your voice or instruments to release hidden tensions, relax the mind, and soothe the body. The sound waves act like gentle waves of energy, loosening tense muscles and stimulating deep relaxation. With each note, you connect to your body's innate harmony, creating a symphony of healing and calm.

1. Preparation: Begin in a quiet, serene space where you can fully relax. Sit or lie down in a comfortable position and take several deep breaths. Imagine your body as a symphony orchestra, where every muscle and organ plays its own unique melody.

2. Choosing the Sounds: Select a sound tool that resonates gently, such as bells, tuning forks, a crystal bowl, or even your own voice humming a soothing tone. Ensure the sound is soft and harmonious, as if it were caressing your body from within.

3. Connecting to the Body: Identify the area in your body that holds tension or discomfort—whether it's your shoulders, back, or knees. This is your focus, the "soloist" in your bodily symphony that needs special attention.

4. Sound as a Therapist: Bring your sound tool close to the chosen area. If using bells, softly ring them near the tension point. If using a crystal bowl, play it gently while focusing its vibrations on the tense or painful area. As the sound envelops the body, visualize its tones penetrating through the layers of muscles and tissues.

5. Vibrations that Heal: Picture each sound wave moving through the tightness in your body, breaking apart stagnant energy and softening the tension. The sound is like a river, washing away blockages and leaving behind calm and harmony.

6. Sound Massage: While creating sound near the tense area, gently move the tool in small circles or along the energy pathways. Imagine the sound waves flowing through your body like a massage, soothing pain and restoring balance.

7. Emotional Release: As the physical tension eases, focus your mind on letting go of emotional stress. Picture the sound waves lifting your worries, fears, and stress, leaving you lighter with each tone. Feel the connection between your body and mind aligning with the sound's rhythm.

8. Conclusion: When the session feels complete, rest your hands on the area you've been healing, letting the warmth of your touch and the residual vibrations soothe you further. Take a deep, cleansing breath, feeling the calm and balance resonating through your entire body. The symphony may have quieted, but its healing notes linger, leaving you in a state of peace and renewal.

Body Portals Meditation

This transformative meditation method focuses on three key energy points in the body: the head, where overwhelming thoughts originate; the feet, symbolizing life's forward motion; and the belly, the emotional reservoir where fear, insecurity, and self-sabotage often accumulate.

Through intentional breathing, visualization, and gentle touches, energy flows are harmonized to bring balance, calmness, and empowerment.

1. Begin with Deep Breathing

Close your eyes and allow yourself to breathe deeply. With each inhale, imagine drawing in fresh, renewing energy. With each exhale, feel tension melting away from your body. Gradually, your body becomes weightless, and your mind begins to quieten.

2. Visualize a Starry Landscape

Envision yourself stepping into a mystical landscape where the sky is ablaze with billions of radiant stars. Around you, starry waterfalls cascade in streams of shimmering light, merging into luminous lakes. As the starlight touches your body, feel your muscles release tension and your mind fill with serene, cosmic light. Imagine light paths stretching across the heavens, connecting you to the universal energy of the stars.

3. Portal Touch – Temples

Place your fingertips gently on your temples, the gateways to your mind. Visualize your hands connecting with starlight that flows into your head. With slow, circular movements, guide the light to cleanse your thoughts, dissolving negativity. Feel the energy streaming downward through your neck and shoulders, collecting in your belly, where it forms a radiant starry chakra—a harmonious blend of solar energy (vitality) and starlight (peace).

4. Portal Touch – Behind the Ears

Move your hands to the soft area behind your ears, avoiding the bone. This is an essential point for releasing tension caused by stress or external energetic disturbances. With gentle circular touches, visualize starlight particles entering your body, unraveling tension in your neck and shoulders, and flowing downward into the starry chakra in your belly.

5. Portal Touch – Soles of the Feet
Place your hands on the soles of your feet, gently massaging in circular movements. Imagine your feet touching a starry lake beneath you, where each drop is not just water but pure light energy. Feel this light entering your body through your feet, traveling upward through your legs toward the belly. With each touch, visualize the energy flowing like waves, harmonizing your body.

6. Merge the Energy Flows in the Solar-Star Chakra
Focus your awareness on your belly—the seat of your solar chakra and your personal energy center. Imagine the light energy flowing from your head and feet merging here into a radiant sphere of cosmic power. The glowing ball pulses with life and illuminates your entire body. Feel its warmth spreading through every cell, bringing calmness, strength, and vitality.

Why It Works

This meditation combines physical touch, visualization, and energy alignment to release tension and restore balance. By activating energy flows from the head, feet, and belly, the body becomes an interconnected system, attuned to universal rhythms. Visualizing starlight not only calms the mind but also invokes the soothing energy of the cosmos, aiding in emotional release and restoring inner strength. With each session, you build a powerful connection between body, mind, and the infinite energy around you.

Transfer of Physical Stress to Natural Elements: A Ritual of Healing

The connection between humans and the natural elements of Earth, often referred to as Lady Gaia, has been celebrated across cultures and centuries. From ancient legends to modern research, nature has always been viewed as a source of profound healing. The practice of transferring physical stress to natural materials—like paper, wood, stone, water, or earth—is not only symbolic but deeply rooted in the principles of somatic release, psychological catharsis, and connection with the Earth's regenerative forces.

1. The Science of Somatic Release

The human body stores stress physically, creating tension in muscles, joints, and even within cellular structures. The mind and body are inextricably connected, and research in somatic therapy has shown that releasing physical stress often alleviates psychological burdens. By engaging with natural materials during this exercise, you tap into this powerful connection.

• Visualization and the "Vessel" Effect:
As you consciously transfer tension into materials like paper, stone, or water, you create a mental "vessel" for your stress. This visualization allows your body to release the stored tension and replace it with feelings of lightness and relief.

• Water's Role as a Conduit:

Water, often associated with emotional flow in ancient traditions, is particularly effective in stress release. Scientific studies, including hydrotherapy research, have shown that water can promote relaxation, reduce cortisol levels, and improve mental well-being. Visualizing your stress flowing into water mimics its natural properties, carrying away what no longer serves you.

• The Earth as a Stabilizer:
Burying your stress in soil, sand, or even clay connects you to the Earth's grounding energy. From ancient practices like grounding to modern research on forest therapy, the Earth's energy field has been proven to stabilize and rejuvenate human well-being. The Earth not only accepts your burdens but transforms them into life-giving energy—just as it turns fallen leaves into fertile soil.

2. Psychological Catharsis: A Ritual of Transformation

Symbolism is a powerful tool for the mind. When combined with physical actions, it creates a deeper emotional release, or catharsis. This exercise utilizes natural elements to bring symbolic closure to stress, transforming tension into something new and constructive.

• The Fire Element:
Burning materials like paper or wood that you've infused with stress is a symbolic act of purification. Fire, revered in traditions ranging from Vedic ceremonies to Native American rituals, is considered a transformative force. As the flames consume the material, the stress transforms into ash, leaving behind only purity.

This act provides a tangible sense of relief as you watch your burdens dissipate into smoke.

• The Flow of Water:
Releasing your tension into water—whether through immersing a stone in a stream or letting written words dissolve in the ocean—is equally therapeutic. Water's symbolism spans cultures: in Greek mythology, the River Lethe erased memory and pain, while Japanese onsen bathing rituals promote purification. Watching the water carry your stress away mirrors this ancient understanding, offering a deep sense of relief.

• Earth's Transformative Power:
Burying materials infused with stress connects you to the regenerative energy of the Earth. Ancient cultures believed the Earth absorbed human emotions and transformed them into life force, creating a balance. Modern eco-psychology supports this idea, showing that contact with soil and nature reduces stress hormones and fosters emotional resilience.

3. A Ritual for the Elements

To perform this exercise, select the material and element that resonates most with you, and follow these steps:

• For Fire: Write your stresses onto paper or gather dried leaves and burn them in a safe space. Watch as the fire consumes them, symbolizing their transformation into light and ash.

• For Water: Hold a smooth stone in your hands, visualizing your tension flowing into it. Place the stone in a stream or body of water, allowing the currents to carry your stress away.
• For Earth: Write down your burdens, fold the paper, and bury it in soil. Visualize the Earth transforming your stress into fertile energy, creating balance and renewal.
• For Air: Whisper your worries into the wind, feeling the air carry them far away, dispersing them into harmless energy.

Why It Works

This method combines psychological and physiological principles with the healing properties of natural elements:

• Catharsis Through Action: The act of transferring stress provides closure, as your mind and body witness the transformation of tension into something harmless or constructive.
• Connection to Earth's Energies: The elements—earth, water, fire, and air—anchor you in the natural rhythms of life, helping you feel part of something greater.
• Scientific Backing: Studies in eco-therapy and environmental psychology confirm that interacting with nature reduces stress, enhances mood, and promotes overall well-being.
• Ancient Wisdom: Cultures worldwide, from Indigenous ceremonies to Celtic rituals, have used these elements for purification and emotional healing, offering time-tested validation of their effectiveness.

Legends of Gaia's Healing Power

In Greek mythology, Gaia, the primordial Earth goddess, was considered the ultimate nurturer. She absorbed human pain and used it to maintain balance and fertility. Similarly, in Native American traditions, the Earth is viewed as a living being that offers healing and stability to all who honor her. These stories remind us that the Earth is not only a place we inhabit but a source of infinite renewal. By engaging with the elements in this ritual, you do more than release stress; you reconnect with ancient truths about balance and healing. Lady Gaia, in her infinite wisdom, absorbs what no longer serves you, leaving you lighter, calmer, and ready to move forward. This practice bridges modern science with timeless wisdom, inviting you to transform stress into serenity.

Self-Guided Meditation: Transferring Physical Stress to Physical Materials

1. Relaxation and Breathing:
Close your eyes and allow yourself to relax completely. Take deep, steady breaths, feeling the tension begin to dissolve with each exhale.

2. Entering Peace:
With every inhale, feel yourself entering a natural state of trust and peace, as though you are being gently held by the energy of the universe.

3. Connection with Nature:
Visualize yourself surrounded by nature's embrace. Feel Mother Earth

flowing through every cell of your body, nourishing and grounding you.

4. Awareness of Earth's Energy:
Sense the precision and rhythm of Earth's energy as it flows within you, carrying abundance, peace, and harmony. Know that this energy is always accessible to you.

5. Creating a Sacred Space:
Imagine the space around you transforming into a magical sanctuary, filled with soothing Zen energy. This sacred space connects you to the infinite love and abundance of nature.

6. Connecting with the Chosen Material:
Become aware of the physical material you have chosen to work with—whether it's paper, wood, dry leaves, stone, or water. Visualize the connection between yourself and this element as part of nature's cycle.

7. Locating the Stress:
Focus on the areas in your body where tension resides—perhaps your stomach, shoulders, or hands. Recognize this stress as energy you've been carrying for too long and are now ready to release.

8. Beginning the Transfer:
As you focus on the chosen material, imagine the stress leaving your body and flowing into it. See the tension as energy being gently absorbed by the material.

9. Transforming the Energy:
Picture the material receiving your stress and transforming it into cleansing, healing energy. Visualize this natural magic unfolding, leaving you lighter and more free with every breath.

10. Release and Liberation:
Feel the profound sense of liberation as the material absorbs your stress. Experience a wave of calm washing over you, as though a weight has been lifted from your being.

Trust your intuition to guide the next step with the material:
- *Burn it, watching the flames purify and transform the energy.*
- *Let the wind carry it away, releasing your fears into the air.*
- *Bury it, allowing the earth to transform it into nourishment.*

11. Gratitude to Mother Earth:
Thank Lady Gaia for assisting in the transformation of this energy into something nurturing and good for you. Feel her grounding and loving energy supporting you.

12. Return to Awareness:
Take several deep breaths, feeling calm and renewed. Begin to bring your awareness back to the present moment as I guide you:

- *10 ... You feel lighter.*
- *9 ... The room begins to take shape.*
- *8 ... Your body feels grounded and whole.*
- *7 ... You sense peace radiating from within.*

- *6 ... Your breath becomes steady.*
- *5 ... Awareness begins to rise.*
- *4 ... The sacred space transforms back into the room around you.*
- *3 ... Your eyes begin to flutter.*
- *2 ... A deep breath fills you with gratitude.*
- *1 ... Open your eyes, feeling calm, light, and fully at peace.*

This practice invites you to release the burdens you carry, with the help of nature's transformative power, allowing you to step forward with clarity and ease.

Part Four

The Architect's Legacy

Chapter Fifteen

The Brain Reset and Disconnect Technique

Now, let us delve into a transformative technique that serves as a gentle yet profound architect for your mind: the Brain Reset. This method is both swift and effective, operating on a principle often overlooked when it comes to holistic breakdowns, mental fears, trauma, or the overwhelming chaos of modern life—especially when your thoughts feel like an intricate maze, pulling you in every direction at once.

The concept is simple yet profound: our brains thrive on order, sequence, and patterns. When life presents us with a logical flow—1, 2, 3, 4—our minds align comfortably, like a skilled dancer following a familiar rhythm. But when the sequence becomes disjointed, the brain falters. Imagine this: you're given the number 8, 5, 3, 1. Easy, right? But now imagine the sequence expands chaotically—10, 12, 14, 23,000, 533,000, 123,456,789. Suddenly, your brain is bombarded, overloaded, unable to process.

This is precisely what happens when life overwhelms us—emotions, tasks, fears, and responsibilities pile on chaotically. The brain, which craves sequence, buckles under the weight of randomness and uncertainty.

Now, let's introduce the idea of calming—both external and internal.

External Calm: The Nature Connection

Think of the soothing sound of ocean waves or the rustling of leaves in the forest. When we immerse ourselves in nature, these external rhythms bring a sense of calm. The sea's rhythmic lapping, for example, mirrors the kind of sequence the brain loves—repetitive, gentle, predictable.

This is why people flock to the mountains, the woods, or the seaside to find peace. Nature has a way of lending its energy to us, momentarily quieting the chaos within. However, there's a limitation to external calm: it's fleeting.

Imagine spending a serene day by the ocean, feeling utterly at peace, only to return home to a chaotic environment. That external calm vanishes as quickly as it arrived, replaced by the stressors of daily life. It's like borrowing serenity from nature without replenishing it within ourselves.

Internal Calm: The Sustainable Solution

This is where the Brain Reset becomes invaluable. Unlike external calm, which depends on your environment, internal calm creates a reservoir of peace within you. It teaches the brain to reorder itself, to find rhythm amidst chaos.

The first step to understanding internal calm is realizing how your brain interacts with stimuli.

Consider sunlight: for some, its warmth and light bring energy and relaxation. For others, the intensity is overwhelming, leading to irritability or fatigue. The difference lies in how our individual brains process and perceive external stimuli.

The same principle applies to stress: when you train your mind to reset and disconnect from chaotic inputs, you cultivate a calm that doesn't waver with changing surroundings. This isn't about escaping to the sea or hiding in the mountains; it's about building your own sanctuary—an internal haven resilient to life's noise.

Why the Brain Reset Works

The Brain Reset technique works because it reintroduces the brain to order and sequence. When you consciously focus on patterns, breathing, and visualization, you provide the brain with the stability it craves. Over time, this internal calm becomes a default state, no longer reliant on external factors.

By resetting the brain and disconnecting from chaos, you empower yourself to navigate life's complexities with clarity and grace. You become the architect of your inner peace, designing a legacy of calm that sustains you in even the most turbulent moments.

The Dance of the Soul: Comfort vs. Growth

Have you ever stopped to wonder why certain moments, places, or atmospheres fill you with an unexplainable peace? For me, it's the quiet magic of winter—the soft hum of snowfall, the hushed whisper of clouds, and the calm that blankets the world in serene stillness. My soul resonates deeply with this wintry energy. My mother even told me that the night I was born, snow covered the earth in a thick, two-meter quilt, and the paramedics warned that if they couldn't reach the hospital, I might enter the world in the back of an ambulance. Perhaps I'm drawn to winter because it was the backdrop of my arrival—a world already muffled, calm, and slow.

For others, it might be different—a sunny meadow, the rhythmic crash of waves, the buzz of a bustling city, or the companionship of a loyal dog. Each of us has these little sanctuaries, these pockets of existence where our brain naturally finds peace. And the brain, wise as it is, knows how to guide us to these places, signaling when we need them more than ever.

But here's the twist. Have you noticed that the more stressed you feel, the more you're drawn to these peaceful escapes? Suddenly, you crave the forest every weekend, the sea every holiday, or a quiet corner to retreat to as often as possible. Your brain is pleading for a reset. And while there's nothing wrong with seeking solace in nature or other comforting spaces, the underlying message is clear: you are not okay. The problem isn't the sanctuary itself—it's our reliance on it. What happens when the sanctuary is gone? When the waves stop, the sun disappears behind endless clouds, or the forest feels out of reach?

Can you maintain your peace, your energy, your clarity?

This is the ultimate test of life: learning to generate internal calm when external sources are unavailable. True mastery comes when you no longer depend on nature, people, or circumstances to restore your energy. Because while external peace is beautiful, it's fleeting. Relying on it alone limits your ability to manifest your soul's greatest potential.

The Trap of Comfort

Let's talk about comfort zones, those cozy spaces where nothing changes, and everything feels safe. Some people spend their entire lives clinging to routines, yearning for calm and simplicity. They say, "I just want a peaceful life. No drama, no upheaval, just contentment." But here's the hard truth: your soul didn't come to Earth for peace. If it did, it would have stayed in the heavenly realms, where love, light, and endless joy already exist. The soul incarnates not for comfort but for growth—for new experiences, challenges, and expansion. It's like a curious child, eager to touch, see, and try everything.

When life becomes too predictable—when you repeat the same job, the same vacation, the same conversations for years—your soul begins to feel restless. Boredom sets in. Have you ever heard the phrase "died of boredom"? It's not just a saying; it reflects a deeper truth. A life devoid of change, growth, or newness suffocates the soul. This is why some people, even when everything seems "fine," feel an inexplicable emptiness. Their soul craves something more, something different—a new path, a new challenge, a new adventure.

The Soul's Mission

Your soul has a purpose, and it's not to live in stagnation. It came here to explore, learn, and create. Staying in your comfort zone might feel safe, but it's the quickest way to disconnect from your mission. Imagine spending 50 years doing the same thing, day in and day out. What's the point? Why incarnate if you're not going to grow?

Manifestation requires stepping out of that comfort zone. It demands investment in your dreams, your goals, your growth. Those who refuse to push past their fears and routines will never reach their full potential. They'll never know the joy of aligning with their soul's mission, of living a life that feels meaningful and alive.

The Call to Action

So ask yourself: Are you living in alignment with your soul, or are you stuck in the comfort of repetition? Are you embracing the challenges and changes that lead to growth, or are you clinging to the familiar, hoping for peace?
Remember, you didn't come to Earth to stay the same. You came to evolve, to explore, and to create. The journey might be uncomfortable at times, but it's also where the magic of life unfolds. Don't settle for merely existing when your soul is calling you to truly live.

Answer the call. Step into the unknown. Your soul is waiting.

The Art of Balancing Inner and Outer Peace

Life often feels like a winding road with both smooth stretches and sharp turns. When external impulses calm us—whether it's the rustling of leaves, the sight of snow, or the hum of a bustling city—our brain finds brief sanctuaries. But as I mentioned earlier, external peace is fleeting without internal balance. This brings us to an important question: what happens when you combine both?

Imagine blending the serenity of your external safe spaces with the grounded strength of your inner peace. What could be more harmonious than creating a union between the outside world's calming essence and the quiet resilience that comes from within? This is the essence of holistic calm.

To explore this further, let me introduce a simple yet transformative method.

The Method: Recognizing Peaceful Corners and Danger Levels

On page 168, you'll find a table that categorizes peaceful corners and ranks their danger levels on a scale from 1 to 10. This tool helps you assess your brain's perception of stressors and prioritize where your energy goes.

Think of it this way:

- Danger Level 10: Financial troubles might feel insurmountable to

someone, creating overwhelming pressure.
• Danger Level 3: Another person, facing the same financial challenges, might shrug it off, saying, “This is temporary; I’ve dealt with worse.”

The difference lies in how our brains perceive and store emotional imprints. Your brain’s danger scale is built from your personal experiences, memories, and emotional conditioning.

Understanding Perception: Why We React Differently

Let’s consider a situation: a family member falls ill. The mother might perceive it as a 10 on the danger scale, imagining the worst-case scenario. Meanwhile, the father might rate it as a 3, thinking, “We’ll figure this out.”

Why the difference? It’s because our brains don’t interpret challenges the same way. Your brain forms its scale based on your life’s unique emotional blueprint.

For instance:

• A person who has faced financial hardship for years may have adapted and no longer perceives it as a high-priority stressor.
• Someone else, encountering financial difficulty for the first time, may feel as though the world is crumbling.
This divergence in perception is critical to understand because it affects how we react to life’s challenges.

Your peaceful corner	Level of 'danger' from 1 to 10

Science Speaks: The Role of Emotional Imprints

Psychological research has consistently shown that the brain's response to stress is deeply tied to past experiences. Studies in neuroscience reveal that when we experience an event, our brain records not just the facts but also the emotional weight of the moment.

For example, the amygdala, the brain's fear center, tags emotional experiences with intensity. Over time, these tags influence how we perceive and respond to future challenges. A person with positive reinforcement in the past might approach stressors with calm and resilience, while someone with unresolved trauma might feel overwhelmed.

Why This Matters

Understanding your brain's perception of stress is the first step in reclaiming control over your emotional reactions. By combining external soothing elements with intentional internal practices, you can recalibrate your brain's response to life's challenges.

This is where the meditation for peaceful corners comes into play. It's a guided practice designed to help you:

- Identify your personal peaceful corners—both external and internal.
- Assess and reframe your brain's danger levels.
- Create a bridge between external calm and internal strength.

The Architect's Reflection

So, the next time life throws you a curveball, pause and reflect:

- What danger level does your brain assign to this challenge?
- How can you merge external peace with internal resilience to navigate the situation?

Remember, your brain is your architect. By understanding how it perceives and prioritizes stress, you can shape a life where challenges become stepping stones, not roadblocks. The power lies in your hands—and your mind.

Navigating the Peaceful Corners: Building Your Inner Sanctuary

Why do we react so differently to life's challenges? It all stems from the emotional imprints left by our past experiences. Each reaction, whether calm or chaotic, is shaped by these imprints, and they dictate how our brains perceive and prioritize danger.

Take, for instance, the dynamic between two people facing the same situation. One trusts implicitly, believing that the angels or life itself will find a way, while the other is riddled with worry, convinced that the weight of the world rests on their shoulders. One remains calm, while the other frets endlessly, asking, "How can you not be worried?" The truth lies somewhere in between—worry won't solve the problem, but unwavering trust often seems too idealistic.

This is where self-awareness steps in. By understanding your personal triggers and the things that can pull you out of distress, you can build your own "peaceful corners" — a toolbox of calming strategies unique to your soul.

Step 1: Identify Your Triggers

Start by listing the things that throw you out of balance emotionally, mentally, or physically. These are your danger zones. Write down at least 20, or as many as you can think of. For example:

- A looming deadline at work
- Financial uncertainty
- Conflict with a loved one
- A health concern

Each of these represents a situation that unsettles your inner peace. Assign a "danger level" to each trigger, from 1 to 10, based on how much it disrupts your calm.

Step 2: Find Your Peaceful Corners

Next, identify the activities, places, or people that naturally calm you. These are your sanctuaries, your sources of external peace. Examples might include:

- Listening to music that transports you to another world
- Walking by the sea or in the forest
- Hugging your dog or spending time with animals.

- Sitting in a favorite café and people-watching
- Immersing yourself in a musical or theater performance

Each person's peaceful corner is unique. For some, the bustling energy of a city might bring them calm, while for others, only solitude in nature will do. Assign a "danger level" to each corner as well—some may be for minor stresses (a level 2), while others may be your refuge in times of major upheaval (a level 10).

Step 3: Acknowledge External vs. Internal Peace

While external sources of calm are valuable, they are not a permanent solution. Relying solely on external factors—be it nature, music, or even a loved one—is like borrowing energy. It soothes you temporarily but does not address the root cause. This is where self-reliance and internal peace come in.

To truly build an unshakable foundation, you must transition from being dependent on external calm to becoming a source of calm within yourself. Imagine becoming an energy pillar, radiating stability and peace that transforms your external reality.

Step 4: The Bridge Between External and Internal

Start by using your peaceful corners as a bridge. When you feel stressed, allow these corners to guide you toward calm. But as you do so, begin to cultivate an inner state that mirrors the external calm.

For example:

• When listening to music, focus on the emotions it evokes and bring that feeling inward, so you can access it even without the music.
• When walking in nature, visualize carrying its tranquility with you, as if the forest now lives within your heart.
• When hugging a dog, absorb its unconditional love and channel it back into yourself.
• Sitting in a favorite café and people-watching
• Immersing yourself in a musical or theater performance

Step 5: Build Resilience from Within

As you practice this, you'll find that you no longer need to rely as heavily on external sources. Your brain will learn to replicate those feelings of calm and stability internally. Over time, you'll become less reactive to external triggers and more grounded in your inner sanctuary.

A Word of Caution: Avoid "Energy Addiction"

It's important to note that even external peace can become a crutch. Just as some turn to substances to escape, others rely on external calm to avoid facing their inner turbulence. True mastery lies in finding balance—using external sources as tools, not dependencies.

Your Soul's Mission

Remember, your soul didn't come to this world for stagnation or comfort zones. It came to explore, to grow, and to experience. Staying in the same routine, repeating the same patterns, and clinging to comfort may feel safe, but it's not what your soul truly craves. The expression "dying of boredom" exists for a reason—it reflects the stagnation of a soul that yearns for more.

By identifying your peaceful corners and cultivating inner resilience, you align with your soul's mission. You step into the role of the architect of your life, navigating challenges not with fear, but with grace and intention. Your peaceful corners become the stepping stones, leading you to your inner sanctuary—the ultimate destination. And once it is built, no challenge is too overwhelming, no obstacle too great. You are prepared, steady, and unwavering.

The Power of Inner Calm: Teaching Your Brain to Self-Soothe

What is your "danger level"? It's not just a number; it's the emotional intensity you feel in a given moment. Panic might rank as a 10, anxiety as a 9, and rage as an 8. Everyone has their triggers—finances, health, family, or work. When you feel panic bubbling to the surface, the first step is to pause and reflect: Is this reaction proportionate to the situation, or has my mind amplified it?

The challenge lies in how we react. When panic strikes, you may instinctively reach for external sources of comfort—a walk by the sea, a hug from your dog, or a moment in nature. While these are powerful tools for external calm, they are not always practical. You can't always rush to the sea or escape to the mountains when stress overwhelms you. This is where internal self-soothing becomes essential.

The Danger of Draining External Energy

While external sources like animals, children, or even nature can bring temporary relief, relying on them comes at a cost. Have you ever hugged your dog and felt your mood lift? While it may have soothed you, the animal often absorbs your stress, which can affect its well-being over time. The same applies to children—they may brighten your spirits momentarily, but you unintentionally offload your emotional burdens onto them, leaving them drained.

This cycle of seeking external relief isn't sustainable. Even nature, as healing as it is, can only do so much. When we rely entirely on the outside world to soothe us, we risk depleting not only our environment but also ourselves. True peace comes from learning to create that calm within.

The Role of Meditation: Turning the Process Around

What if, instead of running to external sources for comfort, you could teach your brain to find the same peace within? This is where meditation comes in—a tool that allows you to recreate your "peaceful corners" internally.

Imagine this: You're overwhelmed, and your brain tells you it needs the sea to calm down. Instead of driving 100 kilometers to the coast, you sit down, close your eyes, and access the same serenity through meditation. You visualize the waves, the salty breeze, and the rhythmic crash of water on the shore. Your brain believes it is there, soaking in the calm, and your body responds by relaxing, just as if you were physically present.

This practice not only saves you from the physical and emotional exhaustion of seeking external solutions, but it also teaches your brain that the peace it craves is already within you. Over time, this internal process becomes your go-to method, reducing your dependency on external factors.

The Long-Term Impact of Internal Self-Soothing

When you master this technique, everything changes. You no longer cling to the hope of an external escape that may not come soon enough. You stop borrowing energy from others or from nature. Instead, you generate your own calm and share it with the world around you. This internal shift transforms you into a creator, a manifestor who can shape life's circumstances rather than being shaped by them.

Why is this so powerful? Because it puts control back in your hands. Instead of reacting to life's challenges, you respond with clarity and grace. You teach your brain that it is capable of managing stress, no matter the situation.

The Key to Transformation

This meditation technique is more than just a practice; it's a life-altering mindset. It retrains your brain to recognize that external peace is only a reflection of the inner calm you can cultivate. By turning inward, you unlock a resilience that makes you less reliant on the unpredictable forces of the outside world.

Imagine carrying the sea, the mountains, or the embrace of a loved one within you—always accessible, no matter where you are or what you face. This shift doesn't just calm you; it empowers you to manifest your goals and dreams with unshakable confidence.

A New Way Forward

So, the next time your danger level spikes, remember: you have the tools to find calm within. Practice this meditation. Teach your brain to turn inward. And witness your life transform, one moment of inner peace at a time. This isn't just a technique—it's a pathway to freedom, resilience, and the boundless potential that lies within you.

Meditation: Brain Reset and Energy Restart

A Journey Into Silence and Renewal

1. Turning Off Thoughts:
Sit comfortably, close your eyes, and take a slow, deep breath in. As you exhale, visualize your thoughts floating away like clouds in the sky. One by one, let them dissolve into the horizon until there's only a vast, clear expanse—an emptiness of pure peace.

2. Turning Off Sounds:
Tune into the sounds around you—cars, voices, distant hums. With every exhale, imagine turning one sound off, as if adjusting a volume knob. Begin with the loudest, gradually moving to subtler noises, until a profound silence surrounds you.

3. Turning Off the Presence of Others:
Visualize the presence of people around you fading. Like dimming a radio signal, feel their energy gently receding. In this space, you are completely alone—free and centered in your own stillness.

4. Turning Off Physical Sensations:
As you breathe deeply, imagine your physical sensations slowly dissolving. Your body becomes weightless, formless, and free. Each muscle unwinds, leaving behind a floating essence untethered by physical limits.

5. Turning Off Light:
Picture all the light around you dimming until darkness wraps you in its

quiet embrace. This darkness is not empty—it's full of peace, a cocoon where you can finally let go.

6. Turning Off Time:
Imagine time itself pausing. There's no past pulling you back, no future pulling you forward—only the present moment exists. Feel the infinite calm of timelessness.

7. Turning Off Gravity and Space:
Now, feel gravity release you. Your body gently lifts, floating effortlessly in a realm where weight and space lose their meaning. You are light, free, and infinite.

Adding Sounds and Awakening Energy

1. The Sound of Birds:
Slowly, the sound of birds begins to echo in your awareness, their melodies soft and harmonious. Visualize vibrant birds soaring across a radiant sky, their wings carrying beams of light that gently touch and rejuvenate you.

2. The Resonance of Instruments:
Subtle notes from musical instruments flow into your space, vibrating through your cells like ripples in a still lake. Each tone massages your body, awakening dormant energies and filling every fiber with life.

3. The Flow of Water:
The soothing sound of water emerges—a gentle stream flowing with grace. Picture this water cleansing your inner world, washing away tension, and infusing you with nature's harmony. It connects you to life's ever-renewing cycle.

4. The Song of Angels:
Finally, a celestial melody unfolds—the tender voices of Angels singing from realms beyond. This sound wraps you in a warm, luminous energy, filling your heart with peace and love. Let their heavenly song guide you deeper into relaxation, into a place where your thoughts find serenity and your spirit finds renewal.

Your New Beginning

Feel your energy refreshed, your spirit light, and your mind open. This practice teaches you to disconnect from the noise and chaos of life, allowing you to find strength and calm within. Every sound you've heard, every sensation you've felt, becomes part of a rhythm that empowers you to face life anew—peaceful, resilient, and alive.

Part Five

Constructing Love

Chapter Sixteen

The Sanctuary of Kindred Souls

Life, at its core, is a shared experience. No matter how much we strive for independence, nothing meaningful is ever truly accomplished alone. Whether it's building a career, navigating challenges, or simply finding peace, the presence of others—our kindred souls—plays a pivotal role.

These are the people who stand beside us in our darkest moments, the ones who understand without judgment and offer unwavering support. Yet, in the chaos of life, we sometimes forget the profound impact they have. We stumble, feeling isolated, when in truth, we are surrounded by connections waiting to anchor us.

The Power of Connection

Think of someone in your life who always stands by you, unwavering in their presence. Perhaps it's a partner, a friend, or a family member. They are the ones who ease your struggles without invalidating your feelings. Their support isn't about providing solutions but about journeying with you, reminding you that you're never alone.

I've experienced this deeply with Michael, my husband. He has been my unwavering anchor during the most challenging chapters of my life. I remember the profound grief that enveloped me when I lost Tara, my beloved dog—not just a pet but a soul companion, a piece of my heart. Many couldn't grasp the depth of my sorrow, dismissing it as too much, too long. But Michael never judged, never wavered. He simply stood beside me, holding space for my pain, allowing me to grieve in my own way, with patience and understanding that only true love provides.

It's not just the physical presence of a kindred soul that matters. It's their energy, their unwavering belief in you, and their ability to make you feel seen and understood.

When Physical Presence Isn't Possible

But what happens when your kindred soul isn't physically there? Perhaps they're navigating their own challenges or simply aren't available at the moment you need them most. This is where the concept of the higher self comes in—a connection that transcends the physical.

Through meditation, you can tap into this deeper bond. Imagine meeting your kindred soul in an ethereal space where their higher self offers guidance and support. It's not bound by the limitations of the earthly world but exists as a source of pure connection and understanding.

This practice doesn't just provide temporary relief; it helps you build resilience and strength. Over time, you'll find that the qualities you admire in your kindred soul become part of you, allowing you to navigate life's challenges with greater ease.

A Journey Toward Inner Strength

While the presence of kindred souls is invaluable, the ultimate goal is to cultivate that same strength within yourself. The meditation to connect with your kindred soul's higher self is a stepping stone—a way to access the support you need while learning to become your own anchor.

Take a moment to think about the people who have supported you through life's ups and downs. What qualities do they bring? How do they make you feel? And now, consider this: what would it mean to embody those qualities yourself?

This journey isn't about becoming self-sufficient to the point of isolation. It's about recognizing that while external support is a gift, true strength comes from within. And through this, you'll find that your connection to others deepens, not because you need them but because you appreciate them for who they are.

Moving Forward

Life's challenges will come, but you don't have to face them alone. Whether through the physical presence of a kindred soul or the deeper connection to their higher self, you have access to the support you need. And as you strengthen this bond, you'll discover an even greater power within yourself.

Let this be a reminder: the connections you cherish are not just a source of comfort; they're a reflection of your own capacity to love, support, and endure. Use them as a guide, and in time, you'll find that the strength you seek has been within you all along.

The Importance of Soul Connections in Meditation

When you are restless or in need of support, connecting with a soul companion can serve as an anchor, guiding you back to your inner peace. The presence of this person reminds you that you are never alone and that someone out there understands and supports you. When you connect with a soul companion in meditation, their energy can help you navigate challenges, doubts, or fears with greater clarity and resilience.

Soul companions often act as inner guides, harmonizing your energy with your true self. By connecting with them, you gain access to their wisdom, which serves as a reflection of your own inner strength and peace. This process is profoundly healing, especially in moments when you feel overwhelmed or lost.

How Mental Connections Work

A mental connection with a soul companion is not just imagination; it's an energetic link rooted in genuine love and connection. Your mind and heart are capable of transcending physical boundaries. When you envision someone who means a great deal to you, your energy aligns with theirs, no matter where they are physically.

Through this connection, you can receive their support and feel a part of something larger than yourself. Such meditations can deepen your self-awareness because soul companions often mirror your own potential, fears, or hidden talents. When you mentally connect with them, you gain the chance to see your situation through the lens of love and support. This helps you uncover deeper insights and experience a profound sense of safety and belonging.

Practical Application Beyond Meditation

While meditation is an excellent way to connect with your soul companions, you can also bring this practice into your daily life. In challenging moments, imagine this person by your side, "hearing" their words of encouragement or wisdom.

It feels as if someone has your back.

And the truth is—they do.

Meditative Support of Soulmates: Connecting with Your Precious Soulmate in Thought

- *Find a Quiet Space: Sit in a calm and serene environment. Close your eyes and take a few deep breaths, allowing yourself to relax completely.*

- *Connect with Your Breath: Inhale deeply, letting peace fill your body. Exhale and release tension, grounding yourself in the present moment.*

- *Visualize an Ethereal Garden: Imagine entering a luminous garden floating above the clouds, with golden-blue glowing flowers lining the pathways and delicate veils of mist gently drifting around you.*

- *Discover the Central Island: Visualize a small floating island with radiant grass and an ancient, moonlit tree at its center, emanating soft, silvery light.*

- *Meet Your Soulmate: Underneath the glowing tree, picture your soulmate as a figure of light, their energy warm, loving, and soothing. Sense their presence as if they are truly with you.*

- *Communicate in Thought: Approach your soulmate and feel their energy embrace you. Share your feelings, ask them a question, or simply express your gratitude. Listen quietly for their response, which may come as a thought, feeling, or image.*

- *Receive Their Support: Feel their loving energy enveloping you, providing wisdom, comfort, or reassurance. Let their light merge with yours, bringing calm and strength to your being.*

- *Express Gratitude: Before leaving, thank your soulmate for their love, guidance, and support. Feel the warmth of their presence lingering within you.*

- *Return to the Present: Slowly open your eyes, carrying the feeling of their presence and love in your heart, as a gentle warmth that gives you strength.*

Chapter Seventeen

How to Calm Others with Meditation

(A beautiful skill if you wish to lead meditations or are already a meditation teacher, or if you want to help your loved ones.)

Leading meditation for others is an extraordinary gift, allowing you to become a portal through which people can reconnect with their inner peace.

However, the key lies in your ability to sense the energy of the group and guide it into a state of calm, no matter how diverse the individuals' experiences or needs may be.

This skill is particularly valuable for meditation teachers or those aspiring to lead meditations for others. By aligning the group energetically, you can anchor specific calming frequencies that allow the space to harmonize. If the energies of participants clash—such as one person being in a state of hostility while another radiates love—the space itself can become disjointed.

Here are some effective techniques:

1. Harmonizing Group Energy – Connecting All into One

At the beginning of the meditation, create a unified energetic flow among all participants. Invite the group to close their eyes and establish a shared rhythm of breathing. Guiding them through synchronized breaths allows individual energies to merge into a harmonious whole. Suggest that they focus on their breath, matching it to the gentle rhythm you lead. This fosters a sense of unity, where everyone feels part of a collective energy.

2. Focusing on the Body – Group Grounding Techniques

To guide the group into a state of calm, encourage them to focus on their physical sensations. For example, direct their attention to the points where their body connects to the floor or chair. This helps them feel grounded and stable. Use reassuring words like, "Feel how the ground beneath you supports you, as if the Earth itself is your strongest ally. Sense the safety and stability of this moment." This grounding fosters a foundation of security, helping participants release stress.

3. Invoking a Shared Peaceful Corner

Since everyone experiences peace differently, use universal calming visualizations. Invite the group to imagine being in a magical garden, by a serene lake, or embraced by a quiet forest. Describe this place with vivid but simple imagery—soft scents of earth, the gentle rustling of wind through leaves, the warmth of sunlight. This allows each participant to connect with their version of peace while remaining within the framework of the shared visualization. Once this shared frequency is established, you can guide individuals to personalize their inner work, while maintaining the collective energy alignment.

4. Closing with Group Grounding

At the end of the meditation, ensure participants feel stabilized and grounded. Invite them to visualize their energy returning to their body, as if roots are growing from their feet deep into the Earth. Use soothing phrases such as, "Your body is your safe home," or "With your presence, you bring peace into your everyday life." Group grounding ensures that every participant feels secure and balanced, carrying the calmness of the meditation into their daily routines.

By guiding others through these steps, you can create an atmosphere where calmness and harmony thrive. This process not only nurtures the individual but also strengthens the collective energy of the group, making every meditation an impactful and transformative experience.

Chapter Eighteen

Gratitude and New Beginnings

Dear Reader,

As we come to the final pages of this journey together, I want to pause and extend my deepest gratitude to you. You've taken the time to not only read these words but to step into the depths of your soul, exploring the intricate designs of your own inner sanctuary. That is no small feat. It requires courage, vulnerability, and a willingness to face the corners of yourself that many shy away from. For that, you have my admiration.

This book was never meant to simply collect dust on a shelf. It was designed as a tool, a guide, and a trusted companion to help you uncover the blueprint of your inner peace. My hope is that within these pages, you've found more than just knowledge—you've found inspiration. Inspiration to create a life that feels true to you, to discover the strength to face challenges with courage, and to build a foundation of calm so steady that no external force can disturb it.

Through the practices, meditations, and insights shared here, my intention has always been to offer you tools to become the architect of your own well-being. Your inner peace is not something that waits for the world to hand it to you; it is something you build—brick by brick, choice by choice, breath by breath.

As you close this book, I hope you feel empowered to continue this work, knowing that peace is not a final destination but a journey. There will be days when it feels easy and days when it feels impossibly hard. But remember, every step you take toward calm and self-understanding is a step toward a stronger, more radiant version of yourself.

Thank you for trusting me to guide you through these pages. It has been an honor to share my own experiences, lessons, and insights with you. My hope is that this book becomes more than just words—that it becomes a bridge, connecting you to the deepest parts of yourself and to the peace that has always been waiting within.

Now, the blueprint is in your hands. May you build a sanctuary within yourself that stands strong through the ever-changing winds of life. And may this sanctuary be a place where love, strength, and serenity flourish.

Visit **christyzettaking.com** to connect and explore more inspiring ideas together.

With heartfelt gratitude and unwavering belief in your journey,
Christy Zetta King

Printed in Great Britain
by Amazon